Multilevel Trust in Organizations

Trust—whether it is between individuals, within teams, or between organizations—is embedded in a multilevel system where the environment and member interactions jointly affect trust at any level. Yet research on trust at different levels of analysis has largely developed independently with little cross-fertilization. This book brings together six chapters that take levels effects explicitly into account to extend our current knowledge about the dynamics of trust.

The chapters examine diverse issues including theoretical and practical implications of multilevel trust, temporal dynamics of trust and how to model it, the mutually influencing relationship between interpersonal trust and organizational structures, and trust in specific contexts such as merger, public market, and economic downturn. By adopting a multilevel approach, these chapters provide more nuanced and realistic insights into trust and yield knowledge that otherwise may be erroneous or unattainable. Together, they illustrate unique challenges and opportunities for understanding trust in the changing landscape of work relationships.

The chapters in this book were originally published as a special issue of the *Journal of Trust Research*.

Ashley Fulmer is an Assistant Professor of Management at Georgia State University, Atlanta, USA. Her research focuses on trust dynamics in organizations and levels of analysis theory and research. She is on the editorial boards of *Academy of Management Review and Personnel Psychology* and an Associate Editor for the *Journal of Trust Research*.

Kurt Dirks is Bank of America Professor of Leadership and Vice Chancellor of International Affairs at Washington University in St. Louis, USA. He is known for his research on the determinants, barriers, and outcomes of trust within organizations and published multiple highly cited and award-winning articles on the topic.

Multilevel Trust in Organizations

Theoretical, Analytical, and Empirical Advances

Edited by
Ashley Fulmer and Kurt Dirks

Routledge
Taylor & Francis Group

LONDON AND NEW YORK

First published in paperback 2024

First published 2020
by Routledge
4 Park Square, Milton Park, Abingdon, Oxon OX14 4RN

and by Routledge
605 Third Avenue, New York, NY 10158

Routledge is an imprint of the Taylor & Francis Group, an informa business

Publisher's Note
The publisher has gone to great lengths to ensure the quality of this reprint but points out that some imperfections in the original copies may be apparent.

Disclaimer
Every effort has been made to contact copyright holders for their permission to reprint material in this book. The publishers would be grateful to hear from any copyright holder who is not here acknowledged and will undertake to rectify any errors or omissions in future editions of this book.

British Library Cataloguing-in-Publication Data
A catalogue record for this book is available from the British Library

ISBN: 978-0-367-46549-0 (hbk)
ISBN: 978-1-03-283932-5 (pbk)
ISBN: 978-1-00-302952-6 (ebk)

DOI: 10.4324/9781003029526

Typeset in Myriad Pro
by codeMantra

Contents

Citation Information

The chapters in this book were originally published in the *Journal of Trust Research*, volume 8, issue 2 (October 2018). When citing this material, please use the original page numbering for each article, as follows:

Introduction
Multilevel trust: A theoretical and practical imperative
Ashley Fulmer and Kurt Dirks
Journal of Trust Research, volume 8, issue 2 (October 2018) pp. 137–141

Chapter 1
Conceptualising time as a level of analysis: New directions in the analysis of trust dynamics
M. Audrey Korsgaard, Jason Kautz, Paul Bliese, Katarzyna Samson and Patrycjusz Kostyszyn
Journal of Trust Research, volume 8, issue 2 (October 2018) pp. 142–165

Chapter 2
Trust development processes in intra-organisational relationships: A multi-level permeation of trust in a merging university
Sari-Johanna Karhapää and Taina Inkeri Savolainen
Journal of Trust Research, volume 8, issue 2 (October 2018) pp. 166–191

Chapter 3
Contextualising the coevolution of (dis)trust and control – a longitudinal case study of a public market
Lena Högberg, Birgitta Sköld and Malin Tillmar
Journal of Trust Research, volume 8, issue 2 (October 2018) pp. 192–219

Chapter 4
Job insecurity, employee anxiety, and commitment: The moderating role of collective trust in management
Wen Wang, Kim Mather and Roger Seifert
Journal of Trust Research, volume 8, issue 2 (October 2018) pp. 220–237

Chapter 5
Trust development across levels of analysis: An embedded-agency perspective
Fabrice Lumineau and Oliver Schilke
Journal of Trust Research, volume 8, issue 2 (October 2018) pp. 238–248

For any permission-related enquiries please visit:
http://www.tandfonline.com/page/help/permissions

Contributors

M. Audrey Korsgaard is a Professor in the Management Department at the Darla Moore School of Business at the University of South Carolina, Columbia, USA.

Paul Bliese is a Professor in the Department of Management at the Darla Moore School of Business at the University of South Carolina, Columbia, USA.

Kurt Dirks is Bank of America Professor of Leadership and Vice Chancellor of International Affairs at Washington University in St. Louis, USA.

Ashley Fulmer is an Assistant Professor of Management at Robinson College of Business, Georgia State University, Atlanta, USA.

Lena Högberg is a Senior Lecturer in Business Administration at Linköping University, Sweden.

Sari-Johanna Karhapää is a Lecturer at Business School in the University of Eastern Finland, Finland.

Jason Kautz is a Doctoral Candidate at the University of South Carolina, Columbia, USA.

Patrycjusz Kostyszyn is a Researcher at the SWPS University of Social Sciences and Humanities, Poland.

Fabrice Lumineau is an Associate Professor in Strategic Management at the Krannert School of Management at Purdue University, West Lafayette, USA.

Kim Mather is a Honorary Research Fellow in Human Resource Management at Keele Business School, UK.

Katarzyna Samson is a Researcher at Wroclaw Faculty of Psychology at the SWPS University of Social Sciences and Humanities, Poland.

Taina Inkeri Savolainen is a Professor of Management & Leadership in the University of Eastern Finland, Finland.

Oliver Schilke is an Assistant Professor of Management and Organizations and an Assistant Professor of sociology (by courtesy) at the University of Arizona, Tucson, USA.

Roger Seifert is a Professor of Industrial Relations at Wolverhampton University, UK.

Birgitta Sköld is a Research Fellow in Business Administration at Linköping University, Sweden.

Malin Tillmar is a Professor in Entrepreneurship at Linnaeus University, Sweden.

Wen Wang is a Reader in HR Management and Employment Relations at the Unveristy of Wolverhampton, UK.

Multilevel trust: A theoretical and practical imperative

Ashley Fulmer and Kurt Dirks

Levels of analysis has long been identified as a key feature of trust (Rousseau, Sitkin, Burt, & Camerer, 1998; Schoorman, Mayer, & Davis, 2007). Trust, as a product and driver of a relationship, by definition involves two or more parties (Ferris et al., 2009). Each party's trust in another is subject to a host of influences across levels of analysis, ranging from dispositions at the individual level and history at the relationship level to norms at the network level and values at the institutional and societal levels, to name a few. The multilevel complexities only increase when we consider trust beyond interpersonal contexts, such as within a team, between different teams, within an organisation, and between different organisations.

Despite this inherently multilevel nature, research on trust incorporating multiple levels of analysis remains limited, while research on trust at different levels of analysis, such as trust in teams and organisations, continues to develop independently with little cross-fertilisation (Fulmer & Gelfand, 2012). This isolation of trust at a single level of analysis ignoring processes and factors from other levels creates non-trivial gaps in our understanding of trust. As a few recent papers show, without a multilevel perspective, we cannot examine critical trust dynamics such as differences in trust within teams and the relationship between interpersonal trust and interorganisational trust. For instance, in a study of teams, De Jong and Dirks (2012) demonstrated how the effect of intra-team trust on team performance is contingent upon the asymmetry in trust between individual dyads. In a study of interorganisational relationships, Vanneste (2016) showed that indirect reciprocity between boundary spanners, where they give to those who give to others, facilitates interorganisational trust between groups of individuals.

In addition to this theoretical imperative, from a practical point of view, a multilevel perspective is necessary to appreciate the role of trust in our changing environment. Individuals and institutions are frequently forced to respond to changes driven by factors at multiple levels. For example, trust in institutions has become more challenging as technology and social media change how people come together and share information. Individuals now have opportunities to engage in both formal and informal relationships through social media, and these relationships can change interpretations of the information from institutions as it shapes the trust that develops. Moreover, individuals and organisations face greater competition, and more rapid change in response to competition, which make trust more difficult to establish and maintain. The need to understand how trust functions in these multilevel frameworks continues to grow as trust holds promise to bridge differences across boundaries and through challenges.

The papers in the current Special Issue

In this Special Issue, we purposefully selected papers that focus on trust involving multiple levels of analysis. These papers adopt the multilevel approach to yield knowledge that otherwise may be erroneous or unattainable. They also reflect the changing landscape of our world, work, and relationships. Together, they address the questions we put forth in the call for papers, including how trust that originates from interpersonal interactions forms at higher levels, such as within and between organisations, how trust is institutionalised at a higher level, and how lower level entities are socialised into trusting, and methodological recommendations for studying trust vis-à-vis levels of analysis. We begin the Special Issue with a paper by Korsgaard, Bliese, Kautz, Samson, and Kostyszyn (2018) focusing on trust dynamics over time. Next, continuing with the attention to time, two papers by Karhapää and Savolainen (2018) and by Högberg, Sköld, and Tillmar (2018) examine trust development in a merger and between public and private sectors. These are followed by Wang, Mather, and Seifert (2018) investigating job insecurity and trust in an economic downturn. We close with a paper by Lumineau and Schilke (2018) examining the link between interpersonal trust and organisational structures. As we discuss below, each of these five papers offers a distinct and yet complementary look into the nature of multilevel trust.

In 'Conceptualizing time as a level of analysis: New directions in the analysis of trust dynamics', Korsgaard et al. (2018) extend a dynamic view on interpersonal trust, which includes the phases of development, dissolution, and restoration. They provide a much-needed review on the theories of interpersonal dynamics and contend that such dynamics are an inherent part of multilevel trust. While much attention has been focused on the multilevel complexities arising from teams and organisations, it is often overlooked that a meaningful level of analysis resides within the individual where an individual's trust can fluctuate overtime. Put differently, the dimension of time itself should be incorporated into investigations of trust if we want to gain a better understanding of the multilevel nature of trust. In addition to this theoretical background, Korsgaard and colleagues offer an illustrative example for an analytical method – discontinuous growth modelling – to examine such within-individual trust dynamics focusing on linear and nonlinear trajectories in different phases of trust. The paper thus provides a rare combination of a theoretical and practical guide to understand trust dynamics over time.

Continuing the focus on trust changes across time, in 'Trust development processes in intra-organisational relationships – a multi-level permeation of trust in a merging university', Karhapää and Savolainen (2018) analyse the process of trust development over the span of 17 years in the context of a merger between two universities. They demonstrate that trust in such a merger develops over time across stages of planning, commitment, execution, and integration and it morphs from being calculation-based to identity-based. Shaped by external factors at the global, national, and local levels such as changing economy and intensified competition, they show that trust in the merger arises from trust between the leaders of the organisations to be merged, spreads to groups of key administrators, and solidifies in the newly merged organisation with new patterns of interactions. The paper applies a multilevel approach to expand on interpersonal trust dynamics to provide a valuable view on trust development in a merger.

Högberg et al. (2018) similarly focus on trust and time but also include the element of control. In 'Contextualising the coevolution of (dis)trust and control – a longitudinal case study of a public market', they examine the relationship between trust and control in interorganisational relationships across the public and private sectors. They show control often leads to distrust in both parties and spreads beyond the focal relationship, but in some cases, control efforts increase trust because the other party rises to meet the additional, more stringent requirements. Further, whether the relationship between trust and control is a positive or a negative one depends on the institutional context such as differences between sectors and business contexts or power differences between parties. The paper highlights the complex relationship between trust, distrust, and control when the relationship takes place across the private and public sectors with drastically different goals and concerns.

So far, the three papers have considered trust as an outcome. The next paper examines trust as a moderator. In 'Job insecurity, employee anxiety, and commitment: The moderating role of collective trust in management', Wang et al. (2018) examine the role of collective trust – when trust is shared among employees – in a challenging economy when employment is increasingly short-term and volatile. Using large-scale workforce data, the authors demonstrate that collective trust in management ameliorates the negative impact of job insecurity at the individual level. Specifically, trust in management that is shared among coworkers attenuates the negative relationship between objective loss of job elements such as pay cuts and reduced hours and organisational commitment as well as the negative relationship between perceptions of possible job loss and job-related anxiety. The paper illustrates the impact of shared trust on how individuals react to changes and how they feel about their own situations.

In the final paper of the Special Issue, Lumineau and Schilke (2018) in 'Trust development across levels of analysis: An embedded-agency perspective' use an embedded-agency approach to advance a model in which they explicate the mutually influencing relationship between trust of individuals within the organisation and the organizational structures. While few studies have examined the impact of organisational structures on trust of organisational members, even less work has considered the role of individuals and their trust in shaping organisational structures. Lumineau and Schilke provide theoretical bases and illustrative examples for both these directions. With this framework in place, they discuss promising areas for future research that can further our understanding of trust from the multilevel perspective within the organisational context. These include the need to differentiate between trust and distrust and the possibility that trust and distrust can form self-reinforcing cycles over time. They also call for collaboration between micro and macro researchers for research on multilevel trust.

Multilevel trust: emerging themes and future directions

Together, the set of five papers provides valuable insights into the multilevel nature of trust as well as promising avenues for future research. Here we identify and discuss three emerging themes from the papers that we think are critical for the further development of multilevel trust research: temporal dynamics, contextual variations, and fluidity between people and place.

First, time is ripe to study the role of temporal dynamics in trust. Korsgaard et al. (2018) offer a compelling case for understanding trust dynamics and a practical guide to one of the methods. Högberg et al. (2018) as well as Karhapää and Savolainen (2018) demonstrate the utility of longitudinal qualitative data analysis. The temporal dimension – whether within-individual or between-organisation – forms a specific level of analysis that can provide important insights that cannot be gleaned at another level. As an example outside the field of trust, research on self-efficacy and performance has shown a positive relationship at the between-individual level but a negative relationship at the within-individual level (Lord, Diefendorff, Schmidt, & Hall, 2010). An explicit consideration of temporal dynamics is particularly important for trust because exchange relationships can go through sudden changes (Ballinger & Rockmann, 2010) that can alter the trust between parties.

Second, attending to the nuances of a given context can provide new insight for theory and more practical relevance. Three of the papers in this Special Issue (Högberg et al., 2018; Karhapää & Savolainen, 2018; Wang et al., 2018) focus on specific contexts. Johns (2006) defined context as 'situational opportunities and constraints that affect the occurrence and meaning of organizational behavior as well as functional relationships between variables' (p. 386). For example, given the differences between economic upturn and downturn and between the public and private sectors, it is possible that trust plays different roles across these contexts. The field has now accumulated a large body of research on trust and it is time to make the differentiation to see when and how trust differs across contexts. We thus recommend researchers to specify the context in which their research takes place, to consider unique trust affordances and constraints of a given context, and to compare trust and its relationships with other factors across contexts when possible.

Finally, there exists some fluidity between people and the environment in which they are embedded. As demonstrated by Wang et al. (2018) as well as Lumineau and Schilke (2018), the differences between people and structure may not be as rigid as typically assumed such that people can change and be part of the structure. Schneider (1987) famously proclaimed, 'the People make the place' and, thirty years later, we continue to strive to understand the fluid relationship between the people and the place and the extent to which the people make the place. As people can form the environment, trust can form a context which is capable of influencing other aspects of the context and also the people. The bottom-up process of how people shape and change their context requires more theorising and investigation, particularly as changes in communication and social media can drastically alter the convergence and emergence processes of emotion, cognition, and behaviours of individuals (Fulmer & Ostroff, 2016).

Given the profound theoretical and practical needs to better understand trust from a multilevel perspective, we are pleased to present the five articles in this Special Issue on Multilevel Trust. They showcase some of the exciting new avenues in the area. By taking levels of analysis explicitly into account, we hope the Special Issue provides a fertile ground for future work on multilevel trust as we continue to develop more realistic knowledge and offer more precise recommendations on trust.

Acknowledgements

We are grateful to the numerous reviewers and Editor-in-Chief Guido Möllering who offered valuable insight and feedback to shape and develop the papers in this Special Issue. We also thank the authors for their contributions to this issue, including those that we were unable to include at this time. Multilevel trust is an area that continues to grow and deserves our attention. As part of this effort, a volume on multilevel trust, edited by Nicole Gillespie, Ashley Fulmer, and Roy Lewicki, is currently underway for the Society of Industrial and Organizational Psychology (SIOP) Frontier Series. The volume is expected to be published in 2020.

References

Ballinger, G. A., & Rockmann, K. W. (2010). Chutes versus ladders: Anchoring events and a punctuated-equilibrium perspective on social exchange relationships. *Academy of Management Review, 35*, 373–391.

De Jong, B. A., & Dirks, K. T. (2012). Beyond shared perceptions of trust and monitoring in teams: Implications of asymmetry and dissensus. *Journal of Applied Psychology*, *97*, 391–406.

Ferris, G. R., Liden, R. C., Munyon, T. P., Summers, J. K., Basik, K. J., & Buckley, M. R. (2009). Relationships at work: Toward a multidimensional conceptualization of dyadic work relationships. *Journal of Management*, *35*, 1379–1403.

Fulmer, C. A., & Gelfand, M. J. (2012). At what level (and in whom) we trust: Trust across multiple organizational levels. *Journal of Management*, *38*, 1167–1230.

Fulmer, C. A., & Ostroff, C. (2016). Convergence and emergence in organizations: An integrative framework and review. *Journal of Organizational Behavior*, *37*, S122–S145.

Högberg, L., Sköld, B., & Tillmar, M. (2018). Contextualising the coevolution of (dis)trust and control – a longitudinal case study of a public market. *Journal of Trust Research*, *8*(2), 192–219.

Johns, G. (2006). The essential impact of context on organizational behavior. *Academy of Management Review*, *31*, 386–408.

Karhapää, S.-J., & Savolainen, T. (2018). Trust development processes in intra-organisational relationships – a multi-level permeation of trust in a merging university. *Journal of Trust Research*, *8*(2), 166–191.

Korsgaard, A., Bliese, P., Kautz, J., Samson, K., & Kostyszyn, P. (2018). Conceptualizing time as a level of analysis: New directions in the analysis of trust dynamics. *Journal of Trust Research*, *8*(2), 142–165.

Lord, R. M., Diefendorff, J. M., Schmidt, A., & Hall, R. (2009). Self-regulation at work. *Annual Review of Psychology*, *61*, 543–568.

Lumineau, & Schilke (2018). Trust development across levels of analysis: An embedded-agency perspective. *Journal of Trust Research*, *8*(2), 238–248.

Rousseau, D. M., Sitkin, S. B., Burt, R. S., & Camerer, C. (1998). Not so different after all: A cross-discipline view of trust. *Academy of Management Review*, *23*, 393–404.

Schneider, B. (1987). The people make the place. *Personnel Psychology*, *40*, 437–453.

Schoorman, F. D., Mayer, R. C., & Davis, J. H. (2007). An integrative model of organizational trust: Past, present, and future. *Academy of Management Review*, *32*, 344–354.

Vanneste, B. S. (2016). From interpersonal to interorganisational trust: The role of indirect reciprocity. *Journal of Trust Research*, *6*, 7–36.

Wang, W., Mather, K., & Seifert, R. (2018). Job insecurity, employee anxiety, and commitment: The moderating role of collective trust in management. *Journal of Trust Research*, *8*(2), 220–237.

Conceptualising time as a level of analysis: New directions in the analysis of trust dynamics

M. Audrey Korsgaard, Jason Kautz, Paul Bliese, Katarzyna Samson and Patrycjusz Kostyszyn

ABSTRACT

Theory on trust development, dissolution, and restoration suggest that trust is a dynamic state that varies in predictable and often systematic ways. Empirical research, however, lags behind the theoretical development, particularly with respect to understanding the trajectory of trust. This article reviews theory on dynamics of trust and some of the limitations in empirical research on these theories. We then describe an established but underutilised longitudinal analytic method that promises to foster significant theoretical refinements. We provide an illustrative example and discuss implications for future research.

Introduction

Trust is a psychological state (Rousseau, Sitkin, Burt, & Camerer, 1998), commonly considered an attitude. Trust has been examined across multiple levels; the individual-level (e.g. Colquitt, Scott, & LePine, 2007; Mayer, Davis, & Schoorman, 1995; McAllister, 1995), the dyadic-level (e.g. Brower, Lester, Korsgaard, & Dineen, 2009; Dass & Kumar, 2011; De Jong & Dirks, 2012; Korsgaard, Brower, & Lester, 2015), the group-level (e.g. Meyerson, Weick, & Kramer, 1996; Simons & Peterson, 2000; Zand, 1972), the organisational-level (e.g. Miles & Snow, 1992), and through a multilevel lens (e.g. Costigan, liter, & Berman, 1998; Gupta, Ho, Pollack, & Lai, 2016). One consistency across all these levels is that trust changes. The nature of change typically occurs in one of two ways. First, theory suggests that trust can develop (or decline) as relationships between parties mature. That is, trust follows a predictable trajectory of formation, dissolution, and restoration, conditional on various individual differences and contextual factors (Fulmer & Gelfand, 2013; 2015). Second, trust may change as the conditions that contribute to or undermine trust vary. These variations in context may include interventions or responses to discrete events (Morgeson, Mitchell, & Liu, 2015) that lead to enduring patterns of change in trust. For example, an organisation may renege on an implied benefit, calling into question the fairness and integrity of the organisation's leadership and undermine trust (Ballinger &

Rockmann, 2010). Such events can lead not only to a discrete change in trust but alter the trajectory: decelerating, accelerating or reversing the trend.

Both developmental and event-based changes require a dynamic, multilevel theoretical and methodological lens. We show that adopting a dynamic lens focusing on the trajectory of trust provides opportunities to formulate and test novel theoretical propositions that cannot be inferred from cross-sectional or two or three-wave longitudinal designs. We propose that by examining trajectories, we can see how the impact of events and changing conditions compound over time or, alternatively, dissipate over time. By examining trajectories, we can more accurately differentiate between (a) relatively trivial events that have an immediate but no lasting effects, (b) events that have a relatively small immediate effect but compound over time to produce meaningful effects, or (c) impactful events that have both an immediate and compounding effect over time.

The goals of this article are to bring the concept of the intra-individual trust trajectory to the forefront of trust theory, encourage the exploration of research questions that feature time in meaningful ways, and provide an analytic framework to help formulate and test hypotheses that focus on trust trajectories. We show that trust data are rarely modelled using statistical approaches that provide clear dynamic interpretations (for an exception see Fulmer & Gelfand, 2015), and we examine how such methodological constraints limit theory formulation and the generation of research questions. We then detail and illustrate an established but underutilised longitudinal analytic method (e.g. Bliese & Lang, 2016; Singer & Willett, 2003) that has the potential to test several compelling and theoretically critical questions about dynamic processes in the trust literature. As this approach is based on mixed effect modelling, it is well-situated to capture individual as well as higher-order effects on trust dynamics. We begin by examining how dynamics are conceptualised in trust theory and research, followed by an overview of how advances in longitudinal analytic methods can be used to test novel propositions regarding the dynamics of trust. Finally, we provide an illustrative example for testing discontinuities in trust trajectories and offer implications for future research.

Intra-Individual change as the basis of multilevel understanding

As noted, trust is a complex, multifaceted construct. It exists at multiple conceptual levels (i.e. individual, dyadic, group, and organisational), is influenced by the social and/or situational context (i.e. social dynamics establish structures that guide trust), and can refer to states as well as processes (i.e. acts as a cause, outcome, or moderator). Taken together, trust is a meso-level phenomena that incorporates psychological processes within group and situational contexts, and is shaped by organisational policies and procedures. As pointed out by Rousseau et al. (1998), trust originates within the individual. Trust can thus be conceptualised within a multilevel framework wherein individuals are nested within dyadic-, team-, and organisational-level processes.

Theory also suggests, however, that trust is a dynamic state, waxing and waning as individuals interact and events reinforce or undermine trust. The dynamics of trust suggests a more elemental level of nesting within the individual: individual-level trust varies across time. As such, our discussion of the dynamic nature of trust as a multilevel construct starts with a framework of intra-individual changes but incorporate a multilevel perspective to explore the influence of higher-order factors.

How change is represented in theory and research on trust

There are numerous theories and models that address change in trust. Broadly, they can be distinguished by those that address the development of trust and those that address disruptive change. Collectively, the relevant literature captures the formation, dissolution and restoration of trust (Fulmer & Gelfand, 2013). The prevailing theory on development of trust includes stage models of trust formation (Lewicki & Bunker, 1996; Shapiro, Sheppard, & Cheraskin, 1992) and the social exchange perspective on trust spirals (Ferrin, Bligh, & Kohles, 2007; Whitener, Brodt, Korsgaard, & Werner, 1998). Research on disruptive change has focused primarily on trust breach and recovery (Kim, Dirks, & Cooper, 2009; Tomlinson & Mayer, 2009).

Stage models of trust

Stage models of trust posit that the basis of trust changes as the relationship develops across three stages. The first stage, *deterrence-based* (Shapiro et al., 1992) or *calculus-based* (Lewicki & Bunker, 1996) trust, refers to early-stage relationships in which the trustor knows relatively little of the trustee personally. Trust at this stage is based on how controls and incentives in the situation compel trustworthy behaviour. These controls and incentives may be reflected in norms, rules, roles or formal context. To the extent that the benefits of acting in a trustworthy manner outweigh costs, the trustor can be confident that the trustee will act accordingly. The second stage is *knowledge-based trust* in which trust is based on the knowledge accumulated over repeated interactions of the trustee's goodwill and ability. This phase involves a sense-making process wherein the trustor attributes actions and outcomes to the trustee. Thus, shifting from calculus-based to knowledge-based trust involves a shift in the focus from situational factors to individual agency for behaviour. The third stage is *identification-based* trust wherein trustors come to believe that the trustee's values and interests are aligned with their own. This stage also involves sensemaking, in that the trustor makes deeper inferences about the trustees' character and values as enduring causes of the trustee's behaviour.

While not explicitly characterised as progressing in stages, McAllister (1995) posited a similar distinction in bases of trust such that trust is likely to be based on beliefs about reliability and dependability, which he termed cognitive trust, and on mutual care and concern, which he termed affective trust. Cognitive trust roughly corresponds to knowledge-based trust, as it is influenced by direct experience with the trustee fulfilling obligations. Affective trust roughly corresponds to identification-based trust given that it results from extended interaction and exchange of social benefits and, thus, takes longer to form.

Stage models of trust hold three important implications for the role of time. First, progression through these stages implies a trajectory of trust over time involving growth and transformation (Lewicki, Tomlinson, & Gillespie, 2006). Second, stage models imply dynamic relationships such that the impact of certain predictors and processes of trust change over time (Lewicki et al., 2006). Third, stage models imply that, as trust progresses through stages, it is more resilient to violations. That is, factors that might undermine trust are less impactful over time. Comprehensive tests of stage models are lacking but some evidence exists for each of these implications, which are discussed below.

Transformation of trust

Stage models of development involve discontinuity and transformation, which requires a degree of energy or momentum to achieve (Stubbart & Smalley, 1999). In the case of trust, stage models suggest that trust will grow and subsequently change in some qualitative fashion (Lewicki et al., 2006). Scholars such as Gulati and Sytch (2007) have suggested that individuals become more effective at applying controls and incentives to regulate the trustee's behaviour, resulting in growth in calculus-based trust. When trust shifts from calculus-based trust to knowledge-based trust, the trustee's actions are perceived to be attributable to the trustee, as opposed to resulting from contextual factors such as rules, policies or contracts (Malhotra & Murnighan, 2002; Schilke & Cook, 2015). Such attributions are likely to occur when the trustee's behaviour exceeds the trustor's expectations with sufficient frequency or magnitude such that it shifts the way in which the trustor processes information (Soenen, Melkonian, & Ambrose, 2017). That is, the transition from calculus-based trust to knowledge-based trust suggests that the trustor perceives the other party as increasingly trustworthy. The transition to identification-based trust similarly involves sufficient growth in trust to alter perceptions of the degree of shared values and interests.

Evidence of growth in trust can be inferred from the relationship between trust and length of the relationship, which, according to a meta-analysis is small and positive (Vanneste, Puranam, & Kretschmer, 2014). A handful of longitudinal studies have demonstrated a positive linear trend in trust over time (Halbesleben & Wheeler, 2015; Hill, Bartol, Tesluk, & Langa, 2009; Wilson, Straus, & McEvily, 2006). However, the relationship between time and trust is arguably more complex, both moderated by the quality of the experience (Levin, Whitener, & Cross, 2006) and, as implied in staged development, nonlinear.

For example, van der Werff and Buckley (2017) found evidence of a nonlinear function for trust among organisational newcomers. Their findings indicated that trust grew in early stages, stabilised in the intermediate stage and then increased again in the late stages. One way to view this function is that newcomers initially formed and developed trust to a certain level, at which point it stabilised until sufficient experience accumulated, prompting shift in thinking about trust and stimulating a new wave of growth. The interpretation is consistent with the idea that stage shifts involve reaching a threshold. Gulati and Sytch (2007) proposed such a threshold, positing that there is a point in inter-organisational relationships, after which direct interpersonal experience contributes to trust. Using spline regression, they identified a break point, before which interpersonal interaction did not predict trust and, after which, experience was positively related to trust. This finding is consistent with the shift from calculus-based trust early in an inter-organisational relationship – in which trust is driven largely by safeguards and rewards built into the contract – to knowledge-based trust, in which trust is influenced by cumulative direct experience.

In addition to implying discontinuities in the development of trust, stage models imply a transformation in trust, which may be manifested as change in the scope or conceptualisation of trust (Lewicki et al., 2006). This notion of the transformation of the construct itself harkens back to the concept of gamma change (Golembiewski, Billingsley, & Yeager, 1976), in which a reconceptualization of perceived reality results in a change in the nature as well as degree of a given state. Gamma change may be manifested as a change in the underlying factor structure (Millsap & Hartog, 1988). Webber (2008) found evidence of such a transformation among student teams working together over the course of a semester. She found that the factor structure of initial trust, as measured by cognitive and affective trust, was unidimensional. Employing the same measures at the end of the semester revealed a two-dimensional factor structure corresponding to cognitive and affective trust.

Dynamic relationships

Stage models imply that impact of certain predictors and processes on trust systematically vary over time (Korsgaard, 2018; Lewicki et al., 2006). In calculus-based trust, the key determinants of trust are contextual factors, such as social and/or legal incentives to compel trustworthy behaviour, and individual differences in expectations the trustor brings to the situation, such as propensity to trust. Assuring trustworthy behaviour may require the trustor to monitor and impose rewards and sanctions. In the knowledge-based trust stage, the contextual factors play a weaker role, as behavioural cues regarding trustworthiness become strong predictors of trust. Trustors are likely to engage in active sensemaking at this stage rather than reactive monitoring, characteristic of calculus-based trust. In the identification-based stage, the impact of behavioural cues on trust weakens. Trustors have formed fixed assessments of their partner's trustworthiness and become more likely to focus on addressing the needs of their partner and of the relationship.

One broad proposition that can be derived from stage models is that early in the relationship, context and trustor disposition drive trust whereas in intermediate stages the trustee's behaviour will drive trust and then, in later stages, relational factors will drive trust. Jones and Shah (2016) tested this idea by estimating the change in the variance in trust explained by the trustor, the trustee and the relationship over time. Consistent with knowledge-based and identification-based stages as occurring later in the relationship, they found that the variance accounted for by the trustee and the relationship grew over time. Also in support of this proposition, Levin et al. (2006) found that the trustee's behaviour significantly predicted judgments of trustworthiness during the intermediate stage, but was not related to judgments in early and late stages. They also found that shared perspective – an indicator of identification – predicted judgments of trustworthiness in late-stage relationships but not in new or intermediate relationships.

Further support was obtained in a study of strategic alliance partners by Schilke and Cook (2015). They assessed the degree to which the trustor was familiar with and knowledgeable about the partner, which can be considered an assessment of whether the relationship had progressed beyond the initial stage of calculus-based trust. They found that when familiarity was high, relational factors more strongly predicted trustworthiness than did calculus factors. These findings suggest that in more mature relationships, relational factors are more relevant to maintain trust than calculus factors.

On the other hand, van der Werff and Buckley (2017) obtained a pattern of predictors over time that contradicted predictions from the stage model. In a three-month study of new employees, they found that the relevance of behavioural cues did not change over time. Further, rule-based trust cues that should build calculus-based trust – and therefore should be most relevant in early stages – were predictive of trust in later stages.

Trust resilience

Stage models also imply that as trust progresses through stages, it is more robust to violations. That is, the impact of factors that might undermine trust weakens over time. Early-stage trust is presumably more fragile, characterised by high vigilance and intolerance of violations of trust. Events early in the relationship can serve to anchor trust and impressions of the trustee (Ballinger & Rockmann, 2010). Research suggest that trust violations occurring earlier in the relationship are more damaging (Lount, Zhong, Sivanathan, & Murnighan, 2008). As experience accrues, impressions of trustworthiness become stronger (Meyerson et al., 1996). These impressions are apt to guide attention to, and interpretations of, trustee behaviour (Delgado-Márquez, Aragón-Correa, Hurtado-Torres, & Aguilera-Caracuel, 2015; Holtz, 2013). Once a strong impression of trustworthiness has formed, vigilance is likely to decline (Fulmer & Gelfand, 2013). Thus, as the relationship progresses, individuals are less likely to attend to cues that run counter to expected behaviour and discount minor violations of trust. When strong relational bonds form, trustors may grant idiosyncratic credit to the trustee and maintain trust despite the occurrence of violations (Fulmer & Gelfand, 2013).

One corollary of theory on resilience is that the trustworthiness can be manipulated to be viewed as either weak or strong trait. The stronger the trait inference of trustworthiness, the more resilient the trust. Support for this prediction was obtained in two studies in which participants were primed to believe that integrity is either an enduring trait or a malleable state. Participants who were primed to think of integrity as a stable trait were less likely to change their perception of their partner's integrity following the revelation of deception (Haselhuhn, Schweitzer, Kray, & Kennedy, 2017). In a similar study, individuals who were primed to think of integrity as a stable trait recovered their trust more rapidly after repeated lapses of trustworthiness (Schweitzer, Hershey, & Bradlow, 2006).

Resilience is also manifested by the impact of relationship experience on trust recovery following a violation. Schilke, Reimann, and Cook (2013) conducted a longitudinal experiment examining the impact of relationship experience on reactions to a trust breach by varying the timing of the trust breach. They found evidence that trust recovered more rapidly and to a higher level if the breach occurred later in the relationship.

Social exchange and trust spirals

A widely-used theory for understanding the dynamics of interpersonal trust is social exchange theory (Ferrin et al., 2007; Whitener et al., 1998). Social exchange theory describes the process of voluntary exchanges of benefits between individuals (Blau, 1964). The offering of a benefit requires trust, because the actor runs the risk that the partner will not reciprocate. If the partner reciprocates in kind, thereby demonstrating trustworthiness, the actor's trust in the partner is confirmed. With repeated mutually beneficial exchanges, trust is likely to grow. As the actor's trust in the partner grows, the actor may seek to extract greater value from the relationship by escalating the exchanges. This process involves offering a benefit of greater value than provided in the past in the hopes of eliciting a reciprocated benefit of greater value from the partner. Even though a level of trust has been established through prior exchanges, escalating the exchange is a risky proposition because the partner may not reciprocate in kind.

An important implication of social exchange theory is that trust leads to cooperation *and* that cooperation leads to trust. This notion is in line with Mayer et al.'s (1995) arguments for a feedback loop between trusting behaviour and interpersonal trust. The reciprocal influence of trust and cooperation reflects the principle that trust, by motivating cooperative behaviour, begets trust (Ferrin, Bligh, & Kohles, 2008; Zand, 1972). Thus, social exchange theory suggests a self-reinforcing process involving repeated cycles of trust and cooperative exchanges wherein trust emerges and builds from the balanced, voluntary exchange of benefits (Korsgaard, 2018). This mechanism would appear to predict either virtuous (trust growth) and vicious (trust decline) cycles. In order for a virtuous cycle to occur, individuals must (a) begin the relationship with a trusting stance, (b) engage with partners who reciprocate with trust and cooperation, and (c) escalate the exchange of benefits as their trust is reinforced. These conditions are supported by both theory and data.

Trusting stance

The initiation of a social exchange relationship involves taking a risk with the other party (Whitener et al., 1998); thus an initial minimal level of trust is needed at the outset of a trusting relationship. Although there is logic and evidence that persons often begin relationships with a distrusting or low trusting stance (Lewicki et al., 2006), theory and research also indicate that it is common for individuals to approach new relationships predisposed to trust (Wicks, Berman, & Jones, 1999). According to a meta-analysis (Johnson & Mislin, 2011) of laboratory trust games (Berg, Dickhaut, & McCabe, 1995), roughly 50% of participants will trust a stranger with a sum of money without a guarantee of any return. Theory on swift or presumptive trust (McKnight, Cummings, & Chervany, 1998; Meyerson et al., 1996) posits that initial trust may exist among strangers based on predisposition and on context cues such as role constraints, group reputation and social categorisation. Indeed, the mere act of voluntarily entering into exchange relationships suggests a minimum level of trust.

Trust growth and the virtuous cycles

Theory and research support the notion that individuals tend to reciprocate, thereby demonstrating their trustworthiness. Two mechanisms motivating reciprocation are obligation to reciprocate and expected reciprocity (Coyle-Shapiro, 2002; Korsgaard, Meglino, Lester, & Jeong, 2010). The obligation to reciprocate refers to when individuals act on the obligation created by the receipt of a benefit. People act on such obligations because they have internalised the norm for reciprocity as a moral norm (Gouldner, 1960). Expected reciprocity refers to the tendency to reciprocate in order to ensure the receipt of future benefits from a partner and to avoid social sanctions of violating the norm of reciprocity. The anticipated benefits of reciprocation – and costs of violating the norm of reciprocity – extend beyond the relationship in question. Based on how they respond to a given trustor, the partner can burnish her reputation for trustworthiness or incur reputational damage within the organisation. Thus, the combined effects of obligation to, and expectations of, reciprocation suggests the partner is likely to reciprocate benefits offered by the trustor, thereby reinforcing the trustor's trust.

This principle has been supported in studies involving multiple-round dilemma games that show that individuals who receive a benefit in one round are likely to reciprocate in the subsequent round (Ferrin et al., 2008; Juvina, Saleem, Martin, Gonzalez, & Lebiere, 2013). Reciprocity forms the foundation of cycles of trust and cooperation. Serva, Fuller, and Mayer (2005) examined dynamics between project management teams and development teams over four cycles of exchanges, focusing on risk-taking in the relationship and cooperative behaviours. They found that one team's cooperative behaviour led the other team to trust more and to subsequently reciprocate with cooperative behaviour. Further, these studies show that the impact of one party's cooperation on the other party's cooperation is mediated by trust. That is, reciprocation reinforces the actor's trust.

Growth in trust and cooperation

The third condition of a virtuous trust cycle – that exchanges of benefits lead to growth in trust and cooperation – has received limited empirical attention. As noted above, evidence from both cross-sectional and longitudinal studies largely supports the proposition that trust tends to grow over time (van der Werff & Buckley, 2017; Vanneste et al., 2014; Wilson et al., 2006). While not formally tested, laboratory research employing trust and dilemma games also suggests positive growth trends in both trust and cooperation over repeated trials (Ferrin et al., 2008). Halbesleben and Wheeler (2015) examined growth in helping and trust between coworkers in established relationships. They found that growth in coworker helping was associated with growth in employees' trust in the coworker, which subsequently led to increased helping directed at the coworker. Similar results have been obtained in a study involving a repeated trust game (Delgado-Márquez et al., 2015). They found that increases in the amount trustors gave were associated with increases in the amount returned. As trust is affirmed, actors may increase or expand the benefits they provide, thereby increasing their partner's trust in them.

In short, there is compelling logic and evidence for virtuous trust spirals characterised by positive trajectories in trust and trusting behaviour. However, there is also ample evidence of violations of trust, lost trust and the growth of distrust. These phenomena are typically studied as discrete events or episodes that create dramatic alterations in the trajectory of trust. The impact of events on discontinuities in trust growth are reviewed below.

Discontinuous change in trust

Stage models and trust cycles suggest a process of growth in trust as the relationship matures, but this process is regularly disrupted or impeded by episodes or events involving a breach of trust (Elangovan & Shapiro, 1998). Events are disruptive to trust because they violate expectations. These events can be positive or negative. Negative events can lead to a trust dissolution phase in which the trajectory of trust stalls or even reverses course (Fulmer & Gelfand, 2013; Korsgaard, 2018). Positive events mitigate the damage of trust violation and assist in a transition to trust restoration, wherein trust reverses course or grows after a violation (Fulmer & Gelfand, 2013).

Trust violations trigger a process of attribution in which the trustor seeks to determine the motives and intentions of the other party (Bijlsma-Frankema, Sitkin, & Weibel, 2015; Kim et al., 2009). This process is triggered when the event raises doubt about the trustworthiness and the costs and benefits of risk taking within the relationship. Strong events – those that are novel, non-routine and important (Morgeson et al., 2015) – can trigger the attributional process. Additionally, persistent occurrence of relatively weak events may trigger the attributional process (Tomlinson & Lewicki, 2006) because consistent behaviour is itself diagnostic of (un)trustworthiness. The ultimate consequences of attributions following negative violations is a downward assessment of trustworthiness and a loss of trust (Kim et al., 2009). Given the self-reinforcing nature of trust, such assessments can lead to a downward spiral of trust.

Similarly, positive events, such as an apology or reparation, can trigger an attributional process wherein the trustor revises perceptions of trustworthiness in an upward fashion (Tomlinson & Lewicki, 2006). As with negative events, this process is contingent on the strength or persistence of positive episodes. If perceptions of trustworthiness are revised, the downward spiral of trust will be disrupted and trust may increase. Thus, the process of trust resolution is somewhat parallel to the process of trust dissolution although resolution is arguably more difficult to achieve. In the context of protracted conflicts, the restoration of trust may benefit from a gradual reciprocation of conciliatory gestures (Tomlinson & Lewicki, 2006).

Empirical limitations to the study of trust dynamics

Theory on the fundamentals of trust dynamics is sound, and as noted above, many of the tenants of trust growth, decline and recovery have been supported empirically. However, the methods generally applied to test propositions about trust dynamics are limited, leaving important insights into trust trajectories untested.

One of the main limitations of empirical research on trust development is that a preponderance of studies are cross-sectional and therefore cannot directly provide information about growth. Many studies have attempted to make inferences about growth by examining the length of relationship as a predictor of trust (e.g. Vanneste et al., 2014), and others have examined cross-sectional proxies of the relationship stage (e.g. Schilke & Cook, 2015). Results from such data, however, are often ambiguous. For example, when examining the length of relationship, the potential attrition of participants creates ambiguity in the findings. Given the opportunity, people will often exit an exchange relationship with an untrustworthy partner. Thus, it may be that time and experience do not lead to growth but, rather, lead to the retention of trustworthy relationships.

Other studies have more directly examined changes in trust by employing pre–post designs (e.g. Schilke, Reimann, & Cook, 2015). But, like cross-sectional studies, such designs do not allow for a direct examination of growth and contextual or individual differences that qualify trust growth. Doing so requires longitudinal data that allow for the modelling of trajectories. For example, we currently know little regarding the *process* of trust dissolution, as most of the evidence of trust breach has been episodic. Research suggests that the negative effects of a given trust breach can be mitigated by the trustees' efforts to manage the narrative for the event (Kim et al., 2009), but the shadow of doubt may colour the interpretation of future interactions. Broader contextual factors, such as performance oriented organisation cultures can heighten vigilance and discourage making allowances for lapses over time (Fulmer & Gelfand, 2013). Thus, while a one-time mitigation of trust breach may be evident, the impact on the trajectory of trust may be deleterious.

Even when longitudinal data exists, examining trajectories may be challenging. A minimum of three observational periods is generally recommended to estimate a linear trajectory, thus studies involving a pre–post design (e.g. Schilke et al., 2015; Webber, 2008) have limited options for examining trajectories over time (see Bodner & Bliese, 2018). Several studies have examined growth by employing three periods (e.g. Hill et al., 2009; Jones & Shah, 2016); however, more than three observational periods are needed to explore some of the more interesting nonlinear trajectories predicted by theory. For example, in a study with four time periods, van der Werff and Buckley (2017) demonstrated that trust temporarily stabilised before increasing again. This pattern, which is consistent with the idea of a threshold of experience is needed before trust develops to the next stage, would not have been detected without the fourth observational period.

The use of longitudinal designs is more prevalent in laboratory studies involving games such as the prisoner's dilemma and trust game (Berg et al., 1995), where it is not uncommon to have as many as 15 trials. In some cases, researchers effectively leverage the robust longitudinal data by using methods designed for these types of data (e.g. Fulmer & Gelfand, 2015). More often than not, though, studies may not be taking full advantage of the data available. For example, some studies have aggregated observation periods reducing the number of within-individual observations to three periods (Ferrin et al., 2008; van den Bos, van Dijk, & Crone, 2012) or truncated the trials to focus on post-event trends (Schilke et al., 2013). In other cases, the trajectories across multiple trials are examined, but growth effects are not formally tested (e.g. Ferrin et al., 2007; Samson & Kostyszyn, 2015; Schilke et al., 2013).

Based on our review, it is clear that understanding dynamic relationships in trust is a rich area of research that poses challenges in terms of theoretical specificity, research design, and analytic approach. Realistically, no single research design or methodological approach will resolve all the issues we have identified. That said, we believe that theory can be significantly refined and advanced by relying more heavily on designs that utilise (a) multiple measurements and (b) analytic approaches that incorporate both developmental and event-based trajectories in trust. Below we discuss how a variant of the longitudinal growth model can be used to provide a more nuanced understanding of changes in trust in designs where researchers can obtain multiple (e.g. six or more) measures over time and where they may or may not chose to incorporate salient events into the process.

Modelling trust dynamics using longitudinal designs and growth modeling

Theorising and testing trust as a dynamic process requires researchers to use longitudinal designs and to employ data analyses that fully leverage the longitudinal data. In many cases, it is useful to consider how changes in trust revolve around intra-individual (or intra-dyadic) trajectories over time. Traditional approaches to examining longitudinal data such as repeated measures ANOVA are limited with respect to studying trajectories. For instance, with 10 measurement occasions, a repeated measures ANOVA could be significant if one of the 10 measurements was extreme: the resulting F-value would indicate that the variance across measures was larger than expected by chance. Stated otherwise, ANOVA is fundamentally about examining overall differences rather than about examining trajectories, though subsequent *post-hoc* trend analyses are often insightful.

In contrast, growth models look at the same data in a way that centeres on understanding trajectories and modelling individual differences in these trajectories (Bliese & Ployhart, 2002; Raudenbush & Bryk, 2002; Singer & Willett, 2003). The questions posed in growth models centere on whether individual trajectories are increasing or decreasing (or staying the same) and whether these individual differences in trajectories can be explained by other factors (e.g. gender, treatment condition, etc.).

Basic growth model

Growth models can be estimated using structural equations modelling (SEM) programmes or by using mixed-effects models.[1] In this article we describe the approach from a mixed-effects model perspective, but both SEM and mixed-effects approaches are functionally equivalent in many situations. In the basic form, the growth model (a) assesses trajectories of change, (b) allows individuals to differ on these trajectories, and (c) includes potential predictors – at the same, or higher levels – for why individuals differ with respect to average levels of the outcome and trajectories. So, for instance, in a basic growth model with six repeated measures, time would be coded as a single vector (e.g. 0, 1, 2, 3, 4, 5). The growth model would use one degree of freedom to indicate whether time had a significant linear relationship with trust; however, we would also test whether each participant had the same linear pattern and then whether participants with specific characteristics (e.g. males) displayed higher trust overall and stronger or weaker trust trajectories. Parenthetically, if time were coded as a factor using 5 degrees of freedom rather than a vector, the mixed-effects model would be equivalent to a repeated measures ANOVA.

In growth models, it is often useful to follow a prescribed set of steps for both analysing and presenting results. One potential set of procedures based on best practices was provided by Bliese and Ployhart (2002). The first step involves estimating a null model to assess the degree to which participants vary on the outcome (i.e. trust). The null model provides an estimate of the interclass correlation (ICC) which can be interpreted as the percent of variance in any one observation that can be explained by properties of the individual.[2]

The second step involves estimating a model with time as a vector. Time as a simple vector of equally spaced intervals (e.g. 0, 1, 2, 3, etc.) captures the linear trend, but can easily be modified to capture quadratic (e.g. 0, 1, 4, 9, etc.) or other forms. The goal of the second step is to determine whether there is a discernible pattern in the trajectories for the sample as a whole. In the context of trust research, the ability to include quadratic and other forms provides the opportunity to test interesting propositions such as tipping points and whether trust reaches an equilibrium (Korsgaard, 2018).

The third step is to determine whether the overall trajectory pattern sufficiently describes all the participants or whether a model that allows each participant to have a unique trajectory provides a better fit to the data. In the context of trust research, this step provides evidence that there are substantive differences between individual trust trajectories that may potentially be explained by individual and contextual differences (e.g. Fulmer & Gelfand, 2013). The fourth step assesses the within-person error structure and adjusts for autocorrelation and/or heteroscedasticity. The fifth step involves adding individual- or higher-level main effects (e.g. gender, treatment condition, etc.) to determine if average levels of the outcome indexed by the ICC can be explained by non-time varying attributes of the person or context. The final step involves adding interactions involving these attributes and time trajectories to determine whether differences in the trajectories can be explained by attributes of the person or context. In the context of trust research, this final step addresses questions about whether dispositional factors (e.g. predisposition to trust) and contextual differences (e.g. competitive vs. cooperative work environments) affect the development and/or decline of trust.

The basic growth model has considerable potential to help answer theoretical questions about trust development given stable individual propensities and fixed circumstances, but this procedure can also be adapted to address disruptions in trust (e.g. Fulmer & Gelfand, 2015) by creating and analysing a block of time-related covariates in a model we refer to as the discontinuous growth model or DGM (Bliese & Lang, 2016; Singer & Willett, 2003). DGM has a relatively long history within the statistical literature, though referred to using a variety of different names (piecewise hierarchical linear model – Hernández-Lloreta, Colmenares, & Martínez-Arias, 2004; Lang & Bliese, 2009; Raudenbush & Bryk, 2002; multiphase mixed-effects model – Cudeck & Klebe, 2002). Bliese and Lang (2016) provide details regarding data structure, analysis steps, and interpretation for a variety of different models including models with two disruptive events.

The discontinuous growth model

The basic DGM framework contains three time-related covariates. The first covariate is time indexed as it was in the growth model (e.g. for six measurement occasions, 0, 1, 2, 3, 4, 5). The second covariate is a dummy code indexed as 0 prior to the event and 1 following the event (e.g. 0, 0, 0, 1, 1, 1 if the event occurred immediately before the fourth measurement occasion). The third covariate is a series of zeros prior to the event followed by a count vector following the event (e.g. 0, 0, 0, 0, 1, 2 if the event occurred immediately before the fourth occasion). When these three time-related covariates are simultaneously included In the model they represent three different aspects of the trajectories. The first vector (time) estimates the linear trajectory before the event. The second vector (the dummy code) estimates the pre–post change associated with the event. The third vector captures the change in the linear trajectory following the event.

These time-related covariates allow one to identify a pre-event trajectory, an abrupt discontinuity at the time the event occurred, and a post-event trajectory. In the context of trust research, this procedure would allow for the estimation of not only the immediate effect of an event such as a trust breach, but its longer-term consequences for trust restoration.

Note that in our example we are explicitly considering cases where our two trajectories (pre-event and post-event) are linear. In many cases, it may be reasonable to consider linear trajectories; however, DGM can be modified to include quadratic or higher-order non-linear terms in either the pre-event or post-event trajectories. For instance, Lang and Bliese (2009) provide detailed coding options in a scenario where learning on a complex task showed an expected negatively accelerating curve. Such applications would be insightful for examining anchoring events (Ballinger & Rockmann, 2010) that transform or redefine trust. DGM can be adapted to accommodate time-varying covariates, to assess the relationships between temporal variation in the predictor (e.g. trustworthy behaviour) and temporal variation in trust. Such procedures could be employed to examine trust spirals. Further, the DGM framework can be extended to examine between-person differences in event experiences as a means to examine how events interact with individual contextual differences. For example, one could test the immediate and long-term impact of trust breach under more or less cognitively-taxing circumstances.

Finally, as noted the DGM can be extended to include multiple discontinuities. For instance, Fulmer and Gelfand (2015) used a variant of the DGM to model two discontinuities when looking at the moderating role of collectivism and group membership on the violations of trust The first discontinuity occurred when the partner (who had been displaying trustworthy behaviour) committed trust violations in the fifth, sixth, and seventh rounds. The second discontinuity occurred when the partner resumed trustworthy behaviour. By utilising the DGM Fulmer and Gelfand (2015) were able to focus both on trajectories associated with violations and trajectories associated with restoration of trust. By including individual-level (i.e. collectivism) as well as dyadic-level (i.e. partner in-/out-group status) factors in their model, Fulmer and Gelfand (2015) were further able to test, and find support for, the hypothesis that collectivist individuals have a more negative immediate response to large as opposed to small violations from an in-group partner and experience slower restoration of trust after the violation.

Incorporating multiple discontinuities can be informative (see Bliese, Adler, & Flynn, 2017); however, the coding and interpretation of these models is complex. Therefore, we elected to conduct a complete re-analysis of a design with a single discontinuity originally published by Samson and Kostyszyn (2015) as an illustrative example of how the DGM is specified and the types of inferences that can be drawn from the DGM.

An illustrative example

Samson and Kostyszyn (2015) utilised a 10 round version of the trust game (Berg et al., 1995) to assess the negative effects of high cognitive load on the development of trust as well as the repair of trust after a trust violation had occurred. To assess the effects of high cognitive load, participants were assigned to one of three conditions in (a) memory load (b) noise load or (c) no cognitive load (control).

At each round of the trust game, participants could give up to 10 units of experimental currency to their partner, which would be tripled. The partner chose what proportion of this amount should be shared with the participant. This study used a computer player to ensure the participants were exposed to the same pattern of trustworthiness behaviour across participants. The study was broken into three stages based on the pre-programed responses of the computer player. In the trust-building stage (trials 1–3), the computer acted in a trustworthy fashion, returning 50% to the participant. In the trust violation stage (trial 4) the computer returned nothing to the participant. In the trust-recovery stage (trials 5–10) the computer again acted in a trustworthy fashion by returning 50%. This design allowed Samson and Kostyszyn to examine the immediate impact of a trust violation (a discrete event) as well as the process of trust recovery following a trust violation.

The researchers conducted a repeated measures ANOVA with condition as a between-subjects factor. They found a significant effect for condition, such that, on average both cognitive load conditions led to lower trust. They also found a significant effect of time. The means, plotted in Figure 1 appear to indicate that trust steadily increased until the

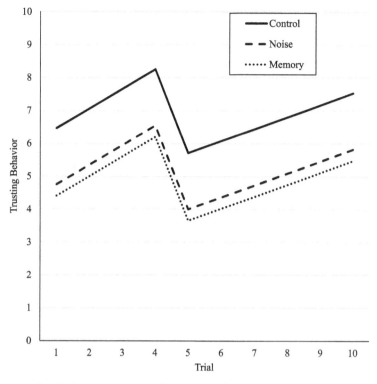

Figure 1. Average level of trust each round by cognitive load condition.

violation round, at which point it dropped substantially then started to increase again. To interpret this effect, Samson and Kostyszyn conducted a series of nine adjacent contrasts (i.e. trial 1 versus 2, trial 2 versus 3, etc.). Four of the nine adjacent comparisons were not significant (3 vs. 4, 6 vs 7, 8 vs. 9 and 9 vs. 10), creating some ambiguity in what was occurring before and after the violation. Thus, while they obtained clear evidence of the disruptive impact of a trust violation, in that there was a significant difference between trials 4 and 5, the pattern of trust growth and the recovery was less clear.

We emphasise that we are not critical of the approach used by Samson and Kostyszyn as ANOVA is a widely used analytic tool. Nonetheless, it is clear from Figure 1 that thinking about the analyses as two trajectories (pre-event and post-event) provides an alternative, compelling way to conceptualise the problem and describe the nature of the results. Furthermore, by applying the discontinuous growth modelling approach to Samson and Kostyszyn's (2015) data, we illustrate how we can extend the original ANOVA findings and provide precise tests of the immediate adverse effect of trust violation and the impact of subsequent trustworthy behaviour on trust recovery.

To begin with, we coded the time vectors, listed in Table 1, as follows. The *Time* variable was sequentially numbered (0 to 9) and represents the rate of trust growth before the violation. The *Trust Violation Event* variable is the second time vector, which was dummy-coded 0 in the first four rounds, after which it was coded as 1. This variable estimates the impact of the violation on change in trust. The *Trust Recovery* variable is the third time vector, which was coded as 0 for the first five rounds, after which it was coded as

Table 1. Coding of the time covariates in the discontinuous growth model

	Trial									
Round	1	2	3	4	5	6	7	8	9	10
Time	0	1	2	3	4	5	6	7	8	9
Trust Violation	0	0	0	0	1	1	1	1	1	1
Trust Recovery	0	0	0	0	0	1	2	3	4	5
Time.A	*0*	*1*	*2*	*3*	*3*	*3*	*3*	*3*	*3*	*3*

an incremental increasing value. This variable represents the change in the trust trajectory. We discuss the *Time.A* variable in Table 1 at a later point.

Following the model building steps outlined above, we first assessed the degree of within-person consistency in trust by estimating the null model. The ICC value of 0.42 for trust indicates that 42% of the variance in any one response can be explained by properties of the participant who provided the rating. An ICC value of 0.42 is high enough to indicate a fair degree of individual consistency but low enough to suggest that individuals are also changing. In our experience, ICC values around 0.50 are common and values between 0.25 and 0.75 suggest both reasonable stability along with some potential to exhibit change.

In step 2 we examine the pattern for the participants as a whole in a baseline DGM. Table 2 provides the results. Notice that the intercept represents trust at time 0 (the first time period). The intercept value of 5.23 represents the average trust at time 0 across all three conditions, thus indicating that in general participants began the relationship with a trusting stance. Table 2 shows that trust increased 0.58 prior to the trust violation and then dropped 3.09 points (in relative terms) when the trust violation occurred. In absolute terms, trust dropped 0.58–3.09 or −2.51 points. This latter value corresponds more closely to the changes in Figure 1. That is, only the Noise condition appears to drop close to 3 points in Figure 1 – the other two groups drop closer to 2 points so an overall absolute drop of −2.51 reflects the average change in Figure 1. Finally, with respect to trust recovery, Table 2 indicates a significant negative effect of −0.21 which again is interpreted relative to time. In absolute terms, the recovery slope is still positive at .37 (0.60 −0.21), but the post-violation slope is significantly lower than the initial slope. Again, Figure 1 clearly demonstrates that the recovery slope is positive despite the negative term in Table 2. Bliese and Lang (2016) provide details on alternative coding for returning absolute values. Table 1 shows one variant labelled *Time.A* that, if substituted for *Time*, returns absolute values for trust violation and trust recovery rather than the relative values returned by *Time*.

In step 3, we estimate between-person differences in the pattern of the trajectories by allowing random variance in the coefficients for each of the time covariates. Table 3 provides the results in rows 2 through 4. The likelihood ratio in row 2 of 51.94 indicates that a

Table 2. Baseline Discontinuous Growth Model

Variables	Est	SE
Intercept	5.23**	0.28
Time	0.58**	0.10
Trust Violation	−3.09**	0.32
Trust Recovery	−0.21*_	0.12

*p < .05, **p < .01, tests are one-tailed, n = 90 participant, 900 observations.

Table 3. Model comparison tests for discontinuous growth models and autocorrelations

Model	df	AIC	BIC	logLik	Test	L.Ratio
1. Random Intercept Model	6	4158.23	4187.01	−2073.11		
2. Random Time	8	4110.28	4148.67	−2047.14	1 vs 2	51.94**
3. Random Time and Trust Violation	11	4054.46	4107.23	−2016.23	2 vs 3	61.83**
4. Random Time, Trust Violation, and Trust Recovery	15	4052.76	4124.73	−2011.38	3 vs 4	9.69*
5. Autocorrelation Error Structure	16	4043.68	4120.45	−2005.84	4 vs 5	11.09**

$*p < .05$
$**p < .01$

model allowing individuals to vary with respect to their pre-event trajectories fits the data significantly better than a model where every participant has the same slope of 0.58. The likelihood ratios in rows 3 and 4 show that individuals significantly varied with respect to how much they immediately dropped at the point of the trust violation (row 3) and with respect to their recovery slope.

To make these findings more transparent we can estimate empirical Bayes values for each participant. The empirical Bayes values for the final model where all time parameters were allowed to randomly vary indicate that participant 1 had an intercept of 3.87, a time slope of 0.65, a drop of 2.10 at the trust violation, and a recovery slope of −.41. In contrast, participant 2 was initially more trusting (5.35 intercept value), was more inclined to trust prior to the violation (time value of 1.03), showed a bigger drop of 6.42 points when experiencing the trust violation, and had a similar recovery slope of −0.40. In our formal modelling we do not explicitly make use of the empirical Bayes values, but Table 3 reflects a formal test of whether the variability for each participant is more extreme than would be expected by chance. If this variability is substantial (as it is) we have a strong empirical basis for trying to explain why some participants dropped 2.10 and others dropped 6.42 at the trust violation (for example).

In step 4 we test for lag-1 autocorrelation (row 5 of Table 3). The change in log likelihood values suggests that we have a better fit to the model when we account for autocorrelation. Model 1 in Table 4 provides the parameter estimates and standard errors when random slopes and autocorrelation are included. Notice that the values are quite similar to the values presented in Table 2 in the initial DGM.

Table 4. Discontinuous growth models

Variables	Model 1		Model 2		Model 3		Model 4		Model 5	
	Est	SE	Est	SE	Est	SE	Est	SE	Est	SE
Intercept	5.21**	0.26	6.47**	0.36	6.52**	0.39	6.46**	0.39	6.51**	0.37
Time	0.60**	0.10	0.60**	0.10	0.58**	0.11	0.60**	0.10	0.60**	0.10
Trust Violation	−3.14**	0.40	−3.14**	0.40	−3.14**	0.40	−3.12**	0.53	−3.14**	0.40
Trust Recovery	−0.23*_	0.12	−0.23*_	0.12	−0.23*_	0.12	−0.23*_	0.12	−0.28*_	0.14
Noise Load (vs Control)			−1.71**	0.47	−1.81**	0.54	−1.57**	0.54	−1.78**	0.48
Memory Load (vs Control)			−2.05**	0.47	−2.12**	0.54	−2.16**	0.54	−2.11**	0.48
Time * Noise Load					0.03__	0.08				
Time * Memory Load					0.02__	0.08				
Trust Violation Noise Load							−0.32	0.61		
Trust Violation * Memory Load							0.24	0.61		
Trust Recovery * Noise Load									0.07	0.12
Trust Recovery * Memory Load									0.06	0.12

$*p < .05$, $**p < .01$, tests are one-tailed, n = 90 participant, 900 observations.

In step 5 we add person-level main effects. Model 2 in Table 4 includes experimental condition and tests whether overall levels of trust were influenced by experimental condition. The overall F for condition (not shown) was significant (F-value = 11.15; $p < .01$). As reported in Table 4, the dummy-coded effects for each cognitive load condition were significant: Noise load vs Control = -1.71 relative difference in trust ($p < .01$); Memory Load vs Control = -2.05 relative difference in trust ($p < .01$). These findings mirror the results reported by Samson and Kostyszyn (2015) based on the ANOVA model and support the conclusion that both memory and noise load had a significant negative impact on average levels of trust across all trials.

In Step 6, we specifically focus on testing whether experimental condition is related to either trajectory (pre-event or post-event) or to the decline at the trust violation. Figure 1 provides relatively little reason to expect differences in trajectories or response to the violation as all three lines are roughly parallel. Our expectations based off a visual examination of Figure 1 are confirmed in that condition is unrelated to the initial trajectory (Model 3); nor is condition related to the decline at the trust violation (Model 4); nor is condition related to the recovery trajectory (Model 5). If results from Models 3 to 5 had been significant we would also have estimated a Model 6 including all interactions simultaneously.

Overall, these analyses provide clear results regarding trust growth and recovery. First, they demonstrate that participants on average began with a trusting stance, and that trust grew steadily as long as the partner behaved in a trustworthy manner. Importantly, the findings indicated that, while subsequent trustworthy behaviour contributed to the recovery of trust, the rate of trust recovery was significantly slower than the initial growth. In short, the results suggest that trust is *rebuilt* more slowly than it is built. This experiment provided a relatively generous opportunity for rebuilding trust in that the partner provided clear and consistent signals of trustworthiness, yet the trajectory for trust recovery was substantially weaker. We could further extend our exploration of post-trajectory trust by including quadratic terms into the model to see if the trust recovered in some non-linear function but based on Figure 1 there is little evidence that we need more than a linear model.

Finally, despite the lack of significant results involving interactions between experimental conditions and the trajectories, the models (Table 3) clearly suggest that the data contain meaningful individual differences in terms of how individuals react to this type of design. In subsequent exploratory analyses we tested age, gender, and propensity to trust as additional individual-level predictors. The results indicated that gender significantly moderated the trust violation ($\lambda_{gender \times trust\ violation} = 2.00$, SE = 0.89, $p < .05$), such that men reacted more strongly and negatively than women. It is noteworthy that gender was not significantly correlated with trust ($\lambda_{gender} = -0.22$, SE = 0.50, n.s.; with gender coded 1 = female), and gender did not interact with time ($\lambda_{gender \times time} = -.23$, SE = 0.23, n.s.) or trust recovery ($\lambda_{gender \times trust\ recovery} = 0.22$, SE = 0.26, n.s.). Thus, there was no evidence of differences in trust growth or trust recovery between men and women. Collectively, these findings suggest that while men reacted more strongly to the violation than did women, gender was not related to trust recovery. As predicted values plotted in Figure 2 illustrate, this pattern of effect results in a persistent decrement in the trust levels of men following the trust violation. This finding suggests the opportunity to understand individual differences in trust dynamics.

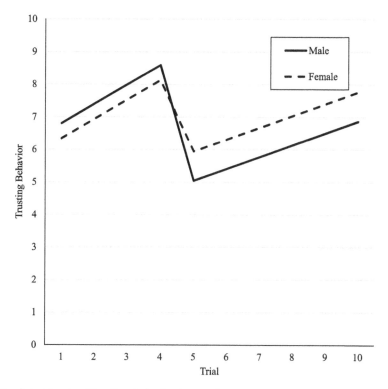

Figure 2. Predicted levels of trusting behavior by gender.

Notes: For illustrative purposes, predicted values within the control condition are reported here. The pattern was parallel for the two cognitive load conditions, as there was non-significant 3-way interaction.

Discussion

The preceding discussion illustrates how growth modelling and the discontinuous growth model could be used to analyse trajectories of trust. As noted above, the models can provide formal tests of trust formation, dissolution and restoration and the factors that contribute to these phases of trust. Further, the models can include a variety of non-linear functions that provide insights into staged development of trust. As with growth modelling, DGM can be adapted to accommodate time-varying covariates, to examine the impact of discrete events on trust spirals: Such procedures could be employed to examine interventions that may break dysfunctional cycles.

In addition, it is important to highlight that growth modelling (including the DGM variant) allows researchers to take a multilevel approach to understanding phenomena and answering research questions. Repeated observations over a period of time constitute the level-1 variables in growth modelling. Individual differences can be included as level-2 variables. Higher-order levels can also be included in the model to account for dyadic, group, and organisation effects. Taken together, this approach allows for an understanding of how multilevel effects interact to influence changes in trust over time (for a deeper discussion on the methodological aspects associated with multiple levels of nesting, see Snijders & Bosker, 1999). Further, newer approaches such as the consensus emergence modelling (CEM; Lang, Bliese, & de Voogt, 2018), may allow researchers to capture the transitions of trust from an intra-individual phenomena to a dyadic, group, and/or organ-isational level phenomena.

An essential requirement for rigorous empirical analysis of trust dynamics is a longitudi-nal design. Such longitudinal designs are amenable to laboratory studies involving dilemma and trust games, which provide an efficient way to conduct a longitudinal study. However, longitudinal research is also feasible in field settings with appropriate measurement. One possibility for relatively short-term longitudinal data collection is experience sampling, which can be collected in intervals as brief as a few weeks. An impor-tant consideration in longitudinal research that involves self-report is the potential for instrumentation and bias. Consequently, short scales, possibly even-item indicators are advisable (Jones & Shah, 2016)

As noted earlier, growth modelling is but one approach to empirically examine dynamics that calls attention to the concept of trust trajectories. We maintain that a basic building block of research on trust dynamics could centre on trajectories of trust over time and that theory can be refined by specifying how these trajectories vary as a function of individual differences, contextual factors, and discrete events. Doing so opens the door to a number of important research questions and theoretical refinements.

Implications

One important implication of viewing conceptual trust dynamics as trajectories is the potential to provide rigorous tests of stage models of trust growth. There are a variety of ways in which a growth pattern may manifest, including a number of exponential and logarithmic functions or as discontinuities in the trajectory. Each of these patterns has a unique theoretical meaning that potentially adds explanatory value to theories sur-rounding the development, decline and recovery of trust; however, because scholars gen-erally have not conceptualised trust in terms of growth trajectories, they may have overlooked several fundamental questions regarding trust. For example, stage models suggest a threshold effect, but we do not know what that effect looks like and what con-stitutes a tipping point. Trust spiral research also holds a number of unknowns. Spirals are not expected to continue indefinitely; relationships are liable to reach some equilibrium beyond which neither trust nor cooperation is likely to increase (Axlerod & Hamilton,1981). We do not currently know when and why trust will stabilise nor why some relationships stabilise at a lower level than others.

Examining trust trajectories may also provide greater understanding regarding which aspects of trust models are dynamic. There are many ways we can represent dynamics in trust models. Stage models specify relationships as dynamic. That is, a predictor may be a strong driver of trust at one stage of the relationship and a weak driver at another stage. For example, written contracts predict trustworthiness in relationships where part-ners do not know each other well, whereas organisation culture is a better predictor of trustworthiness in relationships where partners know each other well (Schilke & Cook, 2015). The trust spiral model specifies relationships between dynamic variables. That is, both trust and its antecedents or consequences change over time. For example, increases in cooperation are associated with increases in trust, but the relationship between trust and cooperation does not necessarily change. Each theoretical perspective downplays the alternative dynamic element, which may obscure the true nature of effects. For example, the trustee's cooperative behaviour may be a strong predictor of trust during the knowledge-based stage, but viewed from the lens of trust spirals, cooperative behaviour should itself be dynamic and dependent on how the trustee is treated by the trustor.

Finally, a more careful consideration of dynamics holds implications for the construct of trust itself. Scholars generally focus on growth in the overall level of trust. But trust may also grow in scope; that is, trust may extend to new activities and situations. Trust as a state is typically considered context-specific: party A trusts party B to do X_1 in situation Y_1. Higher levels of trust would suggest more of X_1 in situation Y_1. Shifts in stages and the escalation of benefits suggest that party A may trust B to do X_1 and X_2 in situation Y_1, or to do X_1 in situations Y_1 and Y_2. To date, scope changes remain unchartered territory. It may be better captured by formative as opposed to reflective measurement models (Edwards & Bagozzi, 2000). Moreover, some theorists argue that trust stage changes represent transformations in trust, which suggests that trust development may involve a fundamental change in what it means to trust (Lewicki et al., 2006). Webber (2008) was a unique example that suggests a gamma change, although the change was not formally tested. These issues may not be amenable to testing in the analytic framework suggested here but represent intriguing directions for further research.

Conclusion

Numerous authors have emphasised the importance of more thoroughly and effectively incorporating time into theory, design, and analysis of topics of interest to organisational behaviour (Bliese et al., 2017; Mitchell & James, 2001; Pitariu & Ployhart, 2010; Ployhart & Vandenberg, 2010; Shipp & Cole, 2015). We believe that trust research, in particular, is ideally situated to embrace these calls for integrating time: as we have shown, many of our influential theories are dynamic and incorporate time and change as key theoretical elements. We contribute to this discussion by showing that if we consider time as trajectories around key events (e.g. trust violations), we potentially open up new and exciting opportunities to refine and advance theory.

Notes

1. Mixed-effects models is a broad term referring to many specific programmes. For instance, PROC Mixed in SAS, HLM, lme in R all represent mixed-effects programmes. Mixed-effects programmes are also sometimes referred to as random coefficient models.
2. In laboratory studies in particular, it may also be informative to calculate a conditional ICC with the time-related covariates and experimental manipulations included to estimate individual differences controlling for experimental design factors (e.g., Bliese, Wesensten, & Balkin, 2006).

Disclosure statement

No potential conflict of interest was reported by the authors.

References

Axlerod, R., & Hamilton, W. D. (1981). The evolution of cooperation. *Science, 211*, 1390–1396.

Ballinger, G. A., & Rockmann, K. W. (2010). Chutes versus ladders: Anchoring events and a punctuated-equilibrium perspective on social exchange relationships. *The Academy of Management Review, 35*(3), 373–391.

Berg, J., Dickhaut, J., & McCabe, K. (1995). Trust, reciprocity, and social history. *Games and Economic Behavior, 10*(1), 122–142.

Bijlsma-Frankema, K., Sitkin, S., & Weibel, A. (2015). Distrust in the balance: Then emergence and development of intergroup distrust in a court of law. *Organization Science, 26*(4), 1018–1039.

Blau, P. (1964). *Power and exchange in social life*. New York: J Wiley & Sons.

Bliese, P. D., Adler, A. B., & Flynn, P. J. (2017). Transition processes: A review and synthesis integrating methods and theory. *Annual Review of Organizational Psychology and Organizational Behavior, 4*, 263–286.

Bliese, P. D., & Lang, J. W. B. (2016). Understanding relative and absolute change in discontinuous growth models: Coding alternatives and implications for hypothesis testing. *Organizational Research Methods, 19*, 562–592.

Bliese, P. D., & Ployhart, R. E. (2002). Growth modeling using random coefficient models: Model building, testing, and illustrations. *Organizational Research Methods, 5*(4), 362–387.

Bliese, P. D., Wesensten, N., & Balkin, T. J. (2006). Age and individual variability in performance during sleep restriction. *Journal of Sleep Research, 15*, 376–385.

Bodner, T. E., & Bliese, P. D. (2018). Detecting and differentiating the direction of change and intervention effects in randomized trials. *Journal of Applied Psychology, 103*, 37–53.

Brower, H., Lester, S., Korsgaard, A., & Dineen, B. (2009). A closer look at trust between managers and subordinates: Understanding the effects of both trusting and being trusted on subordinate outcomes. *Journal of Management, 35*, 327–347.

Colquitt, J. A., Scott, B. A., & LePine, J. A. (2007). Trust, trustworthiness, and trust propensity: A meta-analytic test of their unique relationships with risk taking and job performance. *Journal of Applied Psychology, 92*, 909–929.

Costigan, R., Ilter, S., & Berman, J. (1998). A multi-dimensional study of trust in organizations. *Journal of Managerial Issues, 10*, 303–317.

Coyle-Shapiro, J. A. M. (2002). A psychological contract perspective on organizational citizenship behavior. *Journal of Organizational Behavior, 23*(8), 927–946.

Cudeck, R., & Klebe, K. J. (2002). Multiphase mixed-effects models for repeated measures data. *Psychological Methods, 7*, 41–63.

Dass, M., & Kumar, P. (2011). The impact of economic and social orientation on trust within teams. *Journal of Business & Economics Research, 9*, 1–16.

De Jong, S. B., & Dirks, K. (2012). Beyond shared perceptions of trust and monitoring in teams: Implications of asymmetry and dissensus. *Journal of Applied Psychology, 97*, 391–406.

Delgado-Márquez, B. L., Aragón-Correa, J. A., Hurtado-Torres, N. E., & Aguilera-Caracuel, J. (2015). Does knowledge explain trust behaviors and outcomes? The different influences of initial knowledge and experiential knowledge on personal trust interactions. *The International Journal of Human Resource Management, 26*(11), 1498–1513.

Edwards, J. R., & Bagozzi, R. P. (2000). On the nature and direction of relationships between constructs and measures. *Psychological Methods, 5*, 155–174.

Elangovan, A. R., & Shapiro, D. L. (1998). Betrayal of trust in organizations. *The Academy of Management Review, 23*(3), 547–566.

Ferrin, D. L., Bligh, M. C., & Kohles, J. C. (2007). Can I trust you to trust me? A theory of trust, monitoring, and cooperation in interpersonal and intergroup relationships. *Group & Organization Management, 32*(4), 465–499.

Ferrin, D. L., Bligh, M. C., & Kohles, J. C. (2008). It takes two to tango: An interdependence analysis of the spiraling of perceived trustworthiness and cooperation in interpersonal and intergroup relationships. *Organizational Behavior and Human Decision Processes, 107*(2), 161–178.

Fulmer, C. A., & Gelfand, M. J. (2013). How do I trust thee? Dynamic trust patterns and their individual and social contextual determinants. In *Models for intercultural collaboration and negotiation* (pp. 97–131). Springer: Dordrecht.

Fulmer, C. A., & Gelfand, M. J. (2015). Trust after violations: Are collectivists more or less forgiving? *Journal of Trust Research, 5*(2), 109–131.

Golembiewski, R. T., Billingsley, K., & Yeager, S. (1976). Measuring change and persistence in human affairs: Types of change generated by OD designs. *The Journal of Applied Behavioral Science, 12*(2), 133–157.

Gouldner, A. W. (1960). The norm of reciprocity: A preliminary statement. *American Sociological Review, 25*(2), 161–178.

Gulati, R., & Sytch, M. (2007). Dependence asymmetry and joint dependence in interorganizational relationships: Effects of embeddedness on a manufacturer's performance in procurement relationships. *Administrative Science Quarterly, 52*(1), 32–69.

Gupta, N., Ho, V., Pollack, J. M., & Lai, L. (2016). A multilevel perspective of interpersonal trust: Individual, dyadic, and cross-level predictors of performance. *Journal of Organizational Behavior, 37*(8), 1271–1292.

Halbesleben, J. R., & Wheeler, A. R. (2015). To invest or not? The role of coworker support and trust in daily reciprocal gain spirals of helping behavior. *Journal of Management, 41*(6), 1628–1650.

Haselhuhn, M. P., Schweitzer, M. E., Kray, L. J., & Kennedy, J. A. (2017). Perceptions of high integrity can persist after deception: How implicit beliefs moderate trust erosion. *Journal of Business Ethics, 145*(1), 215–225.

Hernández-Lloreta, M. V., Colmenares, F., & Martínez-Arias, R. (2004). Application of piecewise hierarchical linear growth modeling to the study of continuity in behavioral development of baboons (Papio hamadryas). *Journal of Comparative Psychology, 118*, 316–324.

Hill, N. S., Bartol, K. M., Tesluk, P. E., & Langa, G. A. (2009). Organizational context and face-to-face interaction: Influences on the development of trust and collaborative behaviors in computer-mediated groups. *Organizational Behavior and Human Decision Processes, 108*(2), 187–201.

Holtz, B. C. (2013). Trust primacy: A model of the reciprocal relations between trust and perceived justice. *Journal of Management, 39*(7), 1891–1923.

Johnson, N. D., & Mislin, A. A. (2011). Trust games: A meta-analysis. *Journal of Economic Psychology, 32* (5), 865–889.

Jones, S. L., & Shah, P. P. (2016). Diagnosing the locus of trust: A temporal perspective for trustor, trustee, and dyadic influences on perceived trustworthiness. *Journal of Applied Psychology, 101*(3), 392–414.

Juvina, I., Saleem, M., Martin, J. M., Gonzalez, C., & Lebiere, C. (2013). Reciprocal trust mediates deep transfer of learning between games of strategic interaction. *Organizational Behavior & Human Decision Processes, 120*(2), 206–215.

Kim, P. H., Dirks, K. T., & Cooper, C. D. (2009). The repair of trust: A dynamic bilateral perspective and multilevel conceptualization. *Academy of Management Review, 34*(3), 401–422.

Korsgaard, M. A. (2018). Reciprocal trust: A self-reinforcing dynamic process. In R. H. Searle, A. I. Nienaber, & S. B. Sitkin (Eds.), *Routledge companion to trust* (pp. 14–28). London: Routledge.

Korsgaard, M. A., Brower, H. H., & Lester, S. W. (2015). It isn't always mutual: A critical review of dyadic trust. *Journal of Management, 41*(1), 47–70.

Korsgaard, M. A., Meglino, B. M., Lester, S. W., & Jeong, S. S. (2010). Paying you back or paying me forward: Understanding rewarded and unrewarded organizational citizenship behavior. *Journal of Applied Psychology, 95*(2), 277–290.

Lang, J. W. B., & Bliese, P. D. (2009). General mental ability and two types of adaptation to unforeseen change: Applying discontinuous growth models to the task-change paradigm. Journal of Applied Psychology, *92*, 411–428.

Lang, J. W., Bliese, P. D., & de Voogt, A. (2018). Modeling consensus emergence in groups using longitudinal multilevel methods. *Personnel Psychology, 71*(2), 255–281.

Levin, D. Z., Whitener, E. M., & Cross, R. (2006). Perceived trustworthiness of knowledge sources: The moderating impact of relationship length. *Journal of Applied Psychology, 91*(5), 1163–1171.

Lewicki, R., & Bunker, B. (1996). Developing and maintaining trust in work relationships. In R. Kramer & T. Tyler (Eds.), *Trust in organizations: Frontiers in theory and research* (pp. 114–139). Newbury Park, CA: Sage.

Lewicki, R. J., Tomlinson, E. C., & Gillespie, N. (2006). Models of interpersonal trust development: Theoretical approaches, empirical evidence, and future directions. *Journal of Management, 32* (6), 991–1022.

Lount, Jr, R. B., Zhong, C. B., Sivanathan, N., & Murnighan, J. K. (2008). Getting off on the wrong foot: The timing of a breach and the restoration of trust. *Personality and Social Psychology Bulletin, 34* (12), 1601–1612.

Malhotra, D., & Murnighan, J. K. (2002). The effects of contracts on interpersonal trust. *Administrative Science Quarterly, 47*(3), 534–559.

Mayer, R. C., Davis, J. H., & Schoorman, F. D. (1995). An integrative model of organizational trust. *Academy of Management Review, 20*(3), 709–734.

McAllister, D. J. (1995). Affect-and cognition-based trust as foundations for interpersonal cooperation in organizations. *Academy of Management Journal, 38*(1), 24–59.

McKnight, D. H., Cummings, L. L., & Chervany, N. L. (1998). Initial trust formation in new organizational relationships. *Academy of Management Review, 23*(3), 473–490.

Meyerson, D., Weick, K. E., & Kramer, R. M. (1996). Swift trust and temporary groups. In R. M. Kramer, & T. R. Tyler (Eds.), *Trust in organizations: Frontiers of theory and research* (pp. 166–195). Thousand Oaks, CA: Sage.

Miles, R. E., & Snow, C. C. (1992). Causes of failure in network organizations. *California Management Review, 34*(4), 53–72.

Millsap, R. E., & Hartog, S. B. (1988). Alpha, beta, and gamma change in evaluation research: A structural equation approach. *Journal of Applied Psychology, 73*(3), 574–584.

Mitchell, T. R., & James, L. R. (2001). Building better theory: Time and the specification of when things happen. *Academy of Management Review, 26*(4), 530–547.

Morgeson, F. P., Mitchell, T. R., & Liu, D. (2015). Event system theory: An event-oriented approach to the organizational sciences. *Academy of Management Review, 40*(4), 515–537.

Pitariu, A. H., & Ployhart, R. E. (2010). Explaining change: Theorizing and testing dynamic mediated longitudinal relationships. *Journal of Management, 36*(2), 405–429.

Ployhart, R. E., & Vandenberg, R. J. (2010). Longitudinal research: The theory, design, and analysis of change. *Journal of Management, 36*(1), 94–120.

Raudenbush, S. W., & Bryk, A. S. (2002). *Hierarchical linear models* (2nd ed.). Newbury Park, CA: Sage.

Rousseau, D. M., Sitkin, S. B., Burt, R. S., & Camerer, C. (1998). Not so different after all: A cross-discipline view of trust. *Academy of Management Review, 23*(3), 393–404.

Samson, K., & Kostyszyn, P. (2015). Effects of cognitive load on trusting behavior–an experiment using the trust game. *PloS one, 10*(5), 1–10.

Schilke, O., & Cook, K. S. (2015). Sources of alliance partner trustworthiness: Integrating calculative and relational perspectives. *Strategic Management Journal, 36*(2), 276–297.

Schilke, O., Reimann, M., & Cook, K. S. (2013). Effect of relationship experience on trust recovery following a breach. *Proceedings of the National Academy of Sciences, 110*(38), 15236–15241.

Schilke, O., Reimann, M., & Cook, K. S. (2015). Power decreases trust in social exchange. *Proceedings of the National Academy of Sciences, 112*(42), 12950–12955.

Schweitzer, M. E., Hershey, J. C., & Bradlow, E. T. (2006). Promises and lies: Restoring violated trust. *Organizational Behavior and Human Decision Processes, 101*(1), 1–19.

Serva, M. A., Fuller, M. A., & Mayer, R. C. (2005). The reciprocal nature of trust: A longitudinal study of interacting teams. *Journal of Organizational Behavior, 26*(6), 625–648.

Shapiro, D. L., Sheppard, B. H., & Cheraskin, L. (1992). Business on a handshake. *Negotiation Journal, 8* (4), 365–377.

Shipp, A. J., & Cole, M. S. (2015). Time in individual-level organizational studies: What is it, how is it used, and why isn't it exploited more often? *Annual Review of Organizational Psychology and Organizational Behavior, 2*(1), 237–260.

Simons, T. L., & Peterson, R. S. (2000). Task conflict and relationship conflict in top management teams: The pivotal role of intragroup trust. *Journal of Applied Psychology, 85*(1), 102–111.

Singer, J. D., & Willett, J. B. (2003). *Applied longitudinal data analysis: Modeling change and event occurrence.* New York, NY: Oxford University Press.

Snijders, T. A. B., & Bosker, R. J. (1999). *Multilevel analysis: An introduction to basic and advanced multilevel modeling.* London: Sage.

Soenen, G., Melkonian, T., & Ambrose, M. L. (2017). To shift or Not to shift? Determinants and consequences of phase shifting on justice judgments. *Academy of Management Journal, 60*(2), 798–817.

Stubbart, C. I., & Smalley, R. D. (1999). The deceptive allure of stage models of strategic processes. *Journal of Management Inquiry, 8*(3), 273–286.

Tomlinson, E. C., & Lewlckl, R. J. (2006). Managing distrust in intractable conflicts. *Conflict Resolution Quarterly, 24*(2), 219–228.

Tomlinson, E. C., & Mayer, R. C. (2009). The role of causal attribution dimensions in trust repair. *Academy of Management Review, 34*(1), 85–104.

van den Bos, W., van Dijk, E., & Crone, E. A. (2012). Learning whom to trust in repeated social interactions: A developmental perspective. *Group Processes & Intergroup Relations, 15*(2), 243–256.

van der Werff, L., & Buckley, F. (2017). Getting to know you: A longitudinal examination of trust cues and trust development during socialization. *Journal of Management, 43*(3), 742–770.

Vanneste, B. S., Puranam, P., & Kretschmer, T. (2014). Trust over time in exchange relationships: Meta-analysis and theory. *Strategic Management Journal, 35*(12), 1891–1902.

Webber, S. S. (2008). Development of cognitive and affective trust in teams: A longitudinal study. *Small Group Research, 39*(6), 746–769.

Whitener, E. M., Brodt, S. E., Korsgaard, M. A., & Werner, J. M. (1998). Managers as initiators of trust: An exchange relationship framework for understanding managerial trustworthy behavior. *Academy of Management Review, 23*(3), 513–530.

Wicks, A. C., Berman, S. L., & Jones, T. M. (1999). The structure of optimal trust: Moral and strategic implications. *Academy of Management Review, 24*(1), 99–116.

Wilson, J. M., Straus, S. G., & McEvily, B. (2006). All in due time: The development of trust in computer-mediated and face-to-face teams. *Organizational Behavior and Human Decision Processes, 99*(1), 16–33.

Zand, D. E. (1972). Trust and managerial problem solving. *Administrative Science Quarterly, 17*(2), 229–239.

Trust development processes in intra-organisational relationships: A multi-level permeation of trust in a merging university

Sari-Johanna Karhapää and Taina Inkeri Savolainen

ABSTRACT

This paper introduces a model to study the trust development processes in intra-organisational relationships at multiple levels. The model is applied to explore a multi-level permeation of trust in a merger. More specifically, the empirical study focuses on *how trust develops at different organisational levels in the context of a merger of two universities into one entity*. The study applies a process view using qualitative longitudinal data analysed by a discourse analytical approach. The paper emphasises a dynamic nature of trust development suggesting that the discourse analysis approach applies particularly well to studying trust development as a dynamic process in the longitudinal case study setting. This paper contributes to trust research by adding to contextual process studies on trust development over time at different levels of the organisation. The findings show that trust permeates through the organisation influenced by interaction and the organisation-specific attributes that are manifested in the discursive practices of top management and the individual, group and organisation-level actions.

Introduction

Trust facilitates the strategic actions of an organisation (Korsgaard, Schweiger, & Sapienza, 1995; Minzberg, 1983). A merger, as the strategic action, is one way to accompany the changes, to develop collaborative relations, cultures and ways of acting that aim to affect the competitiveness of an organisation. A merger represents a major change generating uncertainty, insecurity and vulnerability in an organisation (Cartwright & Cooper, 1990; Searle & Ball, 2004; Stahl & Sitkin, 2005). This paper explores *how trust develops at the different organisational levels in the context of a merger* recognising the differing nature of trust at the individual, group and organisational levels (Fulmer & Gelfand, 2012; Kozlowski & Klein, 2000).

Existing research has given limited attention to trust development in a merger and lacks the longitudinal qualitative empirical research of multi-level trust development processes in a merger context (Bachmann & Inkpen, 2011; Searle & Ball, 2004; Stahl & Sitkin, 2005).

Trust development in a merger has been studied (Searle & Ball, 2004) at a micro-level from the perspective of employees who remained in an organisation after a merger. The findings show (Searle & Ball, 2004) that active management in relationships is needed to enhance the cooperation between employees in mergers, highlighting the fairness of the processes and respectful treatment of the employees. This paper provides insights for merger management.

The need for further research in inter-organisational trust development processes at the different organisational levels has been identified (Bachmann & Inkpen, 2011; Currall & Inkpen, 2002; Fulmer & Gelfand, 2012; Schilke & Cook, 2013). The research has shown the important role of trust in the formation of inter-organisational relationships (McEvily & Zaheer, 2006; Ring & Van de Ven, 1994) and across organisational levels (Fulmer & Gelfand, 2012; Schilke & Cook, 2013). The cross-level development of trust in inter-organisational relationships has been studied theoretically (Schilke & Cook, 2013) at the individual and organisational levels. The boundary spanner has been identified (Schilke & Cook, 2013; Vanneste, 2016) as the key operator across organisational levels in order to develop inter-organisational trust. The boundary spanner 'transfers' (Schilke & Cook, 2013, p. 285) trust from the individual-individual level to the individual–organisation level, recognising the dynamic aspect of trust. The paper (Schilke & Cook, 2013) discusses organisational-level attributes which are important inter-organisational trust antecedents but lacks empirical research, which is called for (Bachmann & Inkpen, 2011).

The idea of this paper is to empirically study the multi-level top-down processes of trust development by combining macro and micro perspectives into the organisational context, which is in a state of flux (Langley, Smallman, Tsoukas, & Van de Ven, 2013). This paper applies a model (Karhapää, 2016) which is elaborated by integrating the models of Lewicki and Bunker (1996) and Ring and Van de Ven (1994) enabling to study trust development processes at multiple levels over time by analysing how trust develops based on calculation, knowledge and identification (Lewicki & Bunker, 1996) in the inter- and intra-organisational relationships that appear in processes of negotiation, commitment and execution (Ring & Van de Ven, 1994) during a merger. In this paper, it is explored how interactive mechanisms and the organisation-specific attributes (Schilke & Cook, 2013; Zucker, 1986) drive trust development over time at the different organisational levels between two merging universities. The paper adds a top management perspective on a merger process and illuminates how trust is manifested, engaging in an organisational action as a 'leap of faith' (Möllering, 2006), a merger, and in the top management discursive practices (Fairclough, 1992).

It is often realised that the followed performances of mergers tend to fail in respect to expectations (Fubini, Price, & Zollo, 2007; Riad, 2005; Stahl, Mendenhall, Pablo, & Javidan, 2005). This paper facilitates gaining knowledge for active merger management by providing a more integrated view of trust development at different levels in a merging organisation. It is recognised that an inter-organisational relationship comprises many interpersonal relationships between the merging organisations. The paper suggests that continuous interaction supplemented by efficient and equal organisational practices supports trust to permeate at the different organisational levels in a merger.

Multi-level trust development processes in an organisation

The paper examines how trust develops based on calculation between the heads of top management in the processes of negotiation at an individual level, how trust permeates based on knowledge between the planning groups in the processes of commitment at the group level, and finally how trust permeates based on identification through the merging organisation in the processes of execution at the organisational level. In effect, the paper explores top-down influences from top-level managers to groups and employees, with the source being at the individual level, from which the upper-management-, group-, and employee-level relationships are inferred. While the merger between two organisations as the decision to engage in trusting action as a 'leap of faith' (Möllering, 2006) is made at the individual level on behalf of the organisation, yet the actions take place at the group and organisational levels reflecting interactions and transactions between the merging organisations (Currall & Inkpen, 2002).

Merger challenges the ability and effort of the management to build cooperative relationships in a 'new' organisation (Stahl & Sitkin, 2005). Therefore, fair and equal (Ring & Van de Ven, 1994) organisational processes are important antecedents of cooperation between the members of the 'new' organisation (Korsgaard et al., 1995). Assessments based on efficiency define the most expeditious and least costly governance structure for undertaking a transaction, given production cost constraints, as transaction cost theory suggests (Ring & Van de Ven, 1994). Equity is an equally important criterion for trust development processes in an organisation. Equity does not mean inputs or outcomes are always to be divided equally in an organisation, but rather it means 'fair dealing' (Ring & Van de Ven, 1994, p. 93).

In this paper, trust is defined as 'a state involving confident positive expectations about another's motives with respect to oneself in situations entailing risk' (Boon & Holmes, 1991, 194). The context of a merger comprises organisational interdependence and risk which also are according to Boon and Holmes (1991) the functional core common to the majority of definitions of interpersonal trust. In a merger, the interdependent situation will unfold in which the partner organisation possesses control over the outcomes that the other partner organisation may obtain. The element of risk is generated in this situation because the other partner may not always take the partner organisation's needs and concerns into consideration within the execution of their own actions. The extent of risk involved in a course of action is reflected in the meaning of the outcome, and the expectancy that the other partner will facilitate the particular outcome (also see Boon & Holmes (1991)). In the context of a merger, in which trust and risk are intertwined (Giddens, 1990), trust serves to reduce or minimise potential suspicions or risks in such a strategic action (Fulmer & Gelfand, 2012).

In a merger, the scope of the inter-organisational relationship is comprehensive (Fubini et al., 2007) and makes the trust development between the partners critical. Although individual trust and organisational trust may differ in relation to the trustor (person) and trustee (person, organisation or system; Currall & Inkpen, 2002; Fulmer & Gelfand, 2012; Giddens, 1990), trust in an organisation can be based on trust in the people in an organisation in general (Fulmer & Gelfand, 2012; McEvily & Zaheer, 2006; Nooteboom, 2002). Organisational trust builds on 'confidence in the reliability of a person or system' (Giddens, 1990, 34), with 'system' referring to organisation-level trust. There exists knowledge, positive expectations, ability, traditions, routines, the history of the relationship, integrity, rituals, a certain situation, and benevolence in an organisation which resonate with ontological security and a sense of trust (Fulmer & Gelfand, 2012; Giddens, 1990; Lewicki & Bunker, 1996; Mayer, Davis, & Schoorman, 1995; Möllering, 2013; Schoorman, Mayer, & Davis, 2007).

In this study, trust is seen to permeate through a top-down process, since trust at one organisational level has an influence on trust at another level (Vanneste, 2016). The study applies a process perspective of trust development in work relationships, therefore 'trust is viewed as a dynamic phenomenon that takes on a different character in the early, developing, and "mature" stages of a relationship' according to Lewicki and Bunker (1996, 118), who depict trust being based on calculation, knowledge and identification.

At first, it is analysed how trust emerges at an individual level between the top managers, since a top manager as a boundary spanner is a key individual governing the strategic actions of an organisation (Minzberg, 1973) and influencing inter-organisational trust (Vanneste, 2016). The encounters and interactions between the top managers enable them to gather cues and make conclusions about the trustworthiness of the partner organisation and calculate (Lewicki & Bunker, 1996) the joint future benefits of a merger during the negotiation stage (Ring & Van de Ven, 1994). Trust is initiated based on consideration of the risks and the future benefits associated with making oneself vulnerable to a partner organisation (Currall & Inkpen, 2002; Lewicki & Bunker, 1996; Mayer et al., 1995; McEvily & Zaheer, 2006; Stahl & Sitkin, 2005). The trustworthiness of the partner is predicted on the basis of prior interactions (Möllering, Bachmann, & Lee, 2004).

A party's trust is signified by a decision to engage in action, a merger that allows its future to be determined by the other party (Boon & Holmes, 1991; Currall & Inkpen, 2002) under a condition of risk. Trust 'bridges' risks and may be seen as the basis for risk-taking behaviour and cooperation (Möllering, 2001; Sydow, 2006). In this study, the enabling effect of trust is seen as the momentum for the merger as a 'leap of faith' (Möllering, 2006). The risk is accepted. There is a cognitive process based on interpretation and rational prediction that enables actors to cope with uncertainty and vulnerability (Bachmann & Inkpen, 2011; Möllering, 2006) trust being based on calculation (Lewicki & Bunker, 1996). Possible doubts are suspended and the other party is assumed to be trustworthy.

Secondly, it is analysed how trust develops at the group level in a merging organisation. On the basis of calculation and gathered information based on face-to-face interactions at the individual level between the top managers, the commitment (Ring & Van de Ven, 1994) is made, enabling engagement in an action, the 'leap of faith' (Möllering, 2006) as a merger. In the commitment stage, the terms and the governance structure of the 'new' organisation have to be established (Ring & Van de Ven, 1994). Therefore, the planning groups are nominated including members from both of the partner organisations. By working together and interacting directly with the partner organisation within these planning groups as the boundary spanners, more knowledge (Lewicki & Bunker, 1996) is gathered at the group level. The working role interaction (Ring & Van de Ven, 1994) and gathered knowledge engenders predictability, thus the further 'leaps of faith' (Möllering, 2006) are made. Interaction and knowledge gathering enable trust to permeate at the group level, and thus, builds trust.

Trust can be affected by organisation communication (Nooteboom, 2002) and may also facilitate collaboration between its members (Nooteboom, 2002; Savolainen, Lopez-Fresno, & Ikonen, 2014). Communication and information sharing are important mechanisms to build trust in the context of a merger while there are multiple sources of risk in a merging organisation (Korsgaard et al., 1995; Searle & Ball, 2004). The risk in a merger emerges from the experience of the negative outcomes if the other party turns out to be untrustworthy with opportunistic behaviour. Also, a merger between the equal organisations involves strategic risks related to organisational culture. There are two culturally different organisations to be integrated, and on the other hand, the valuable cultural features of the partner organisations are to be preserved (Fubini et al., 2007).

Employees may face insecurity in their future employment. During the merger process, there are rumours which need to be dispelled in order to reduce employee anxiety (Stahl & Sitkin, 2005). Even though time and circumstances may require the management decisions without the consensus at the group level, the processes used to reach strategic decisions affect the commitment, attachment, and trust of individual group members (Korsgaard et al., 1995; Searle & Ball, 2004). When the members of a group believe that the management of both partner organisations is honest, sincere and unbiased in taking their positions into account, trust is perceived at the group level (Korsgaard et al., 1995).

Thirdly, it is analysed how trust as 'the collectively held trust orientation by members of one organisation toward another organisation' (McEvily & Zaheer, 2006, p. 280) based on identification (Lewicki & Bunker, 1996) develops during the execution of a merger (Ring & Van de Ven, 1994). At this point, the 'new' organisation, with its commitments and rules of action established, the notion of two organisations becoming one is operationalised. The planning groups of a merger had executed their commitments and are integrated back to their own duties within a 'new' organisation. These boundary spanners have gained knowledge of the colleagues of the partner organisation by interacting directly with one another. They are key individuals fostering trust permeation to an intra-organisational level (Vanneste, 2016) within a 'new' organisation. Active management is needed to enable ongoing interaction that serves the interpersonal relationships (Ring & Van de Ven, 1994) to evolve in addition to working role relationships. Thus, trust may permeate from the group level to the organisational level, fostering identification-based trust (Lewicki & Bunker, 1996) to emerge in a 'new' organisation.

Similar organisational industry, geographic location and organisational age serve as important inter-organisational trust antecedents supporting intra-organisational trust to permeate in a merging organisation (Schilke & Cook, 2013). Similarities in these organisation-specific attributes (Bachmann & Inkpen, 2011; Schilke & Cook, 2013; Zucker, 1986) bring familiarity (Gulati, 1995) due to the common background and shared values at the organisational level between the members of the merging organisations. After the execution (Ring & Van de Ven, 1994) of the merger, a common routine begins formulating in a 'new' organisation.

Figure 1 illustrates an integrated view of trust permeation at the individual, group and organisational levels as top-down processes in a merger. The process of a merger and the formation of the 'new' organisation are characterised as the 'leaps of faith' (Möllering, 2006) through interaction (Ring and Van de Ven, 1994) and trust being based on calculation, knowledge and identification (Lewicki & Bunker, 1996). Although there are good reasons to trust the other party, uncertainty and vulnerability are lurking behind the

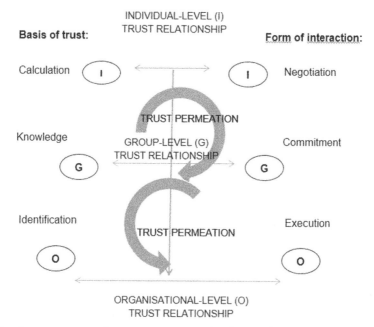

Figure 1. Top-down processes of trust permeation and a 'leap of faith' at the individual, group and organisational levels in a merger.

relationship. Misunderstandings, conflicts and changing expectations may occur, thus continuous interaction is needed to lay out the terms of the organisational relationship supplemented by assessments of the balance of efficiency and equity (Ring & Van de Ven, 1994). When the continuous interaction supported by efficiency and equity becomes routine, the process of trusting (Möllering, 2013) may be generated, applied and maintained in an organisation.

Context of the empirical case study

The empirical part of this study presents one single case (Yin, 2003), the University of Joensuu, located in Eastern Finland. A merger, which can be typed as the horizontal one (Cartwright & Cooper, 1990), brings another university organisation, the University of Kuopio, also located in Eastern Finland, into the picture.

The University of Joensuu, with its eight faculties, had two campuses located in Joensuu and Savonlinna with 8300 students and 1350 staff members. There were five faculties at the University of Kuopio, comprising 6200 students and 1500 staff members (Vihko, 2007). The multi-campus university with four faculties was established with its 15,000 students and 2800 employees and started operating on 1 January 2010. Two universities with 13 faculties merged into a single entity with four faculties. There are two faculties operating solely on the Joensuu campus and the Kuopio campus, and two faculties jointly in both campuses. It takes about two hours to drive by car from one campus to another, which are located 135 km apart geographically.

The merging universities share a common establishment history in Finland, and thus a common organisational age. The establishment of the universities in Eastern Finland during the 1960s was due to the regional and higher-educational policy in Finland at the time (Nevala, 2009; Vuorio, 2006). The universities in Joensuu and Kuopio were both founded in 1966, however, with different profiles. The University of Joensuu specialised in the humanities and education and the University of Kuopio in health sciences (Clark, 2004; Nevala, 2009; Vuorio, 2006).

The case university organisation is contextualised in the global context. Universities in all countries were faced with contradictory external and internal forces of change in the 1990s. Globalisation was an essential concept in the public debate at the end of the 1990s. This was partly a result of changes in society, such as the rise of the global knowledge economy. Universities are expected to support social and economic development more directly perhaps than ever before (Hölttä, 1995; Pinheiro, Geschwind, & Aarrevaara, 2016).

The globalisation discourse reflected the higher education policy at the national level, especially public discussion surrounding the effectiveness of the universities, experienced an acceleration. There was criticism posed towards the magnitude and size of the Finnish universities. Finland was seen to lack universities with international-level research capabilities. The profilisation and specialisation of universities were called for (Kaukonen & Välimaa, 2010).

Furthermore, internationalisation and the European Union play a role in Finnish university politics. There is a groundswell of support for more autonomous universities to take on the goal of reforming university management. The establishment of the 'new' university was part of a major university reform in Finland in 2010 accompanying the structural development of the Finnish higher education sector and The New Universities Act (Yliopistolaki 558/2009) (MinEdu, 2015). The act aims to enhance universities' competitiveness in the international competitive environment by giving universities more economic autonomy and emphasising university management (Karhapää, 2016). Thus, the case university faced two major changes at once; a university reform and a merger.

Methods and analysis

Time is taken into consideration in this empirical case study with the aim to identify processes that enable a more integrated view of trust development at different levels in an organisation (Kozlowski & Klein, 2000), time, interaction and context being the basic elements of a process view (Langley et al., 2013; Möllering, 2013; Savolainen & Ikonen, 2016). Empirically, this study draws on qualitative case study material and the discourse analytical approach (Fairclough, 1992; Phillips & Hardy, 2002) in describing how trust develops in the merging university.

The rector, as the most senior manager in the university organisation, is seen here to be able to influence the thoughts and deeds (van Dijk, 2001) of the university community discursively. The rector's speeches are the important source of organisation communication sharing knowledge through reasoning and building a 'world in common' (Bachmann & Inkpen, 2011; Zucker, 1986) within the merging universities. Discourse enables the rector to influence the implementation of trust development through his speeches. The rector has a unique position that entails gaining information, which enables him to develop a common understanding within the organisation. The rector's status, authority, and unique access to information, place him at the central point in the system, through which significant strategic organisational decisions are made (Minzberg, 1973).

The rector's speeches form the primary research data in this longitudinal single-case study. The rector's speeches as key research data are valuable since the rector is the top manager in a university and plays a role (Ring & Van de Ven, 1994) of the boundary spanner (Perrone, Zaheer, & McEvily, 2003) in a formation of inter-organisational relationship by interacting with the partner university. Boundary spanners interact directly with another organisation as part of their employee roles linking organisational structure to the environment by buffering, moderating or influencing the environment (Aldrich & Herker, 1977; Vanneste, 2016). Boundary spanners, such as the rector and the planning groups of the merger in this case study, are the most relevant employees in the implementation and management of inter- and intra-organisational relationships (Schilke & Cook, 2013).

In this study, it is seen that in the merger process, vulnerability could be made more tolerable and acceptable through top management, the rector in the case university. The management talk may develop trust. The sense of ontological security towards the merging university within the university community and among the stakeholders is strengthened via the rector's discourse. In the data, this is analysed and interpreted from the trust building point of view at the organisational level, and assuming that the employees, students, local, national and global community need trust in the merging university in order to cooperate and gain competitiveness.

The data are analysed by applying a qualitative content analysis (Eriksson & Kovalainen, 2008) to identify themes of the trust development processes at the different organisational levels from the speeches and other theory-based data included. The textual data are categorised according to the stages of a merger of negotiation, commitment and execution (Ring & Van de Ven, 1994). The main themes within these stages of a merger were summarised. This was followed by the identification of the themes discussing and reflecting the basis and nature of trust (Lewicki & Bunker, 1996) at different organisational levels during each stage of a merger (Ring & Van de Ven, 1994). The themes concerning trust development and permeation at different organisational levels are described and analysed.

Trust development processes are interpreted in the rector's speeches adapting the discursive approach (Burr, 2003; Demers, 2007). A discursive approach builds on social constructionism (Berger & Luckmann, 1972) with the idea that language is more than a reflection of reality; rather the language constructs the social reality (Burr, 2003; Phillips & Hardy, 2002). To study language and communication is a way to gather knowledge about the merger process (Burr, 2003; Demers, 2007), to ask what things mean and to make interpretations (Phillips & Hardy, 2002) about how trust developed at the different organisational levels in a merging university.

The interpretation of the data is made on a theoretical basis. The produced description of the trust development process is reported through indirect quotation of the speech. Therefore, the original wordings are not necessarily quoted, yet some particular reporting words are framed. The illustrative excerpts in the speeches are used in order to illuminate and verify the interpretation of trust permeation processes through different organisational levels.

Discourse is understood here as something that is produced, consumed, and circulated in society (Fairclough, 1992). The study aims to describe how the texts, as a form of management speak, empower intra-organisational trust to develop at the organisational level, especially during the merger process by developing positive expectations (Möllering et al., 2004). When analysing the 'discourse-as-discursive-practice' (Eriksson & Kovalainen, 2008; Fairclough, 1992), the attention was paid to speech acts, coherence and intertextuality, all of which situate speech and text into context.

When producing the discourse as the text (Fairclough, 1992) and preparing the speeches, the rector has assumed (per the interview of 2014) that the audience would be more interested in facts than invigorating rhetoric with fewer issues. To give fact-based speeches at the university opening ceremony was a conscious choice of the rector (per the interview of 2014). The rector prepared the speeches as a researcher by gathering ideas and thoughts during the year and formulating a schema for them. The speeches are not edited for publishing purposes, even though the speeches are public. The discourse is consumed (Fairclough, 1992) by the members of a university community and stakeholders who attended a semester opening ceremony. The speech of the rector may be cited in the local and national newspapers and publications. The text consumption by the press was not very eager (also per the interview of 2014). The rector directed his message to the professors and stakeholders, and, of course, to the staff of the university when preparing and giving the speech (per the interview of 2014).

The annual speeches given at the university opening ceremony by the rector are interpreted as an act of interaction and connection, showing a relational, reciprocal gesture towards people in a merging organisation. This indirect reciprocity (Vanneste, 2016) is seen to be manifested annually in the feedback that the rector receives after his speeches from the members of the university organisation. The feedback contains ideas and cues from internal and external environments which are manifested within the intertextuality (Fairclough, 1992) in the speeches. Not being a single individual, but rather the members of the (partner) university as a trustee, the indirect reciprocity is particularly important from an inter-organisational trust perspective (Vanneste, 2016), and especially in the context of a merger.

Data

The data is gathered at the individual level consisting of the speeches of the rector in the case university. The rector as a trustee gives a speech in an annual opening ceremony of the university at the beginning of September, according to specific rituals. A university organisation and the rector representing the university are the objects of trust. The speeches are consumed (Fairclough, 1992) by the trustors, members of the university (staff and students), who are invited to the ceremony, as well as stakeholders including representatives of the Ministry of Education, the church, representatives of the local council, business and 'friends of the university community', as is stated in the speeches.

The longitudinal data of this study covers the period of 17 years (from 1998 to 2014) containing the rector's annual semester opening ceremony speeches (see Appendix 1) and includes 100 pages as primary research data in addition to an interview with the rector. The interview is conducted at the end of the rectorship period in November 2014. The new rector, who started at the beginning of 2015 for five years, had been nominated. There was an ongoing transition process between the new rector and the present rector at the time of the interview. The interview enlightens the inter- and intra-organisational processes retrospectively.

The interview with the rector consisted of a set of questions on three themes (see Appendix 2). The themes aimed to situate talk and text into the context of a merging university. The production process for the speeches, the feedback and reciprocity of the speeches were identified, as well as the text distribution and consumption from the rector's perspective was introduced. The additional data consist of the written histories of the two merging universities, administrative and strategy reports and plans for university reform in Finland, as well as project reports of the merger process.

The data provide in-depth comprehension about the context and process of the merger from the perspective of the case university's rector. The data illuminate the formation of the 'new' university of Eastern Finland out of two studied from the rector's point of view. The rector in question held his top management position for 17 years. He served as a rector at the University of Joensuu from 1998 to 2009 and after the merger, as a rector at the University of Eastern Finland from 2010 to 2014. In other words, only one actor held the rector position during the research period of 17 years. Therefore, this long period of data and the perspective are considered a unique data set within the university management context. The rector's speeches and interview enable researchers to capture and study the multilevel top-down processes of trust development over time in the case university, including theory basis through multiple references in the written speeches.

The rector prepares and writes the speeches himself. The rector's academic identity as a professor and a researcher of human geography is interpreted as being visible in the data, especially at the beginning of the research period, on the basis of the multiple references applied in the speeches. Thus, the speeches contain intertextuality (Fairclough, 1992). The external change forces and interests seem to shape the rector's speeches. The speeches are linked to other texts, ideologies and hegemonies (Fairclough, 1992) such as globalisation, internationalisation and marketisation.

Findings: intra-organisational trust development processes during merger

Next, the findings of the longitudinal qualitative case study are discussed. The trust development processes in inter- and intra-organisational relationships are revealed. It is illuminated how trust permeated from the individual level to the group level, and from the group level to an organisational level in a merging university over time influenced via interaction and organisation-specific attributes, such as similar organisational industry, geographic location and organisational age. It is depicted how trust development is manifested in the organisational action as a 'leap of faith' (Möllering, 2006), a merger, and in the rector's discursive practices.

Trust permeation at the individual level – the rector as a boundary spanner

The rector of the case university has met his colleague of the partner university over the years in official and unofficial occasions. An important source of interaction (interview 2014) was provided since the beginning of the new millennium by the local provincial government in Eastern Finland, which had annually organised informal summer meetings and invited the rectors of the higher education institutes. These informal meetings enabled interaction and communication between the rectors. During these meetings, there was a general discourse of cooperation, but the merger was not stated as an option, until

2005. It seems that interpersonal trust in a negotiation partner at the individual level emerges at the beginning of the new millennium during unofficial meetings.

The actual negotiations aiming toward cooperation were initiated in 2005. The concept of 'merger' was mentioned in the rector's speech at the opening ceremony for the first time also in 2005 inspired by the presentation of the Organisation for Economic Cooperation and Development (OECD) officer. The delegation of Finnish rectors were participating in June 2005 in the international event enlightening the aspects of higher education management organised by the OECD Programme on Institutional Management in Higher Education (IMHE). The IMHE programme officer introduced the list of the programme's five M's: mission, markets, money, management and mergers, concerning the current challenges the university institutes meet. The rector notes (in a 2005 speech) that the list of the programme's five M's reflects the current international university conversation. In a 2005 speech, the rector describes the merger in the case university context:

> Mergers: Forced alliances directed by outsiders are not preferable, but strategic alliances with neighbouring higher education institutes are – as far as there are benefits achieved which are obvious for all the parties. (The 2005 speech)

The discourse contains reasoning and themes of calculus-based trust (Lewicki & Bunker, 1996), since the cooperation is expected to bring benefits to the merging universities. The University of Joensuu and the University of Kuopio are feasible and complementary partners. From the Joensuu University perspective, to be among the best 200 universities in the world will not be possible without research in medicine. On the other hand, from the perspective of the University of Kuopio, the strong fields in the University of Joensuu, such as natural sciences and forestry, would complement research in the 'new' organisation after the merger. Additionally, the University of Joensuu is efficient in its educational mission (Nevala, 2009).

The criterion of equity (Ring & Van de Ven, 1994) is apparent in discourse as the benefits are to be achieved by 'all the parties'. The merger of the two university organisations occurs between equals in this case study. The aim of the merger was to gain synergy (Cameron & Green, 2004). There is the potential ability of two organisations to be more successful when merged than when they are apart. The gains of the merger are achieved through strengthened education and research. There are also expected cost reductions through economies of scale and financial synergies.

Earlier, the macro-level external driving forces for change were recognised in the rector's discourse. The social context of the universities was transforming in the late 1990s. At the end of the 1990s and at the beginning of the new millennium, the discourse containing themes of international competition and need for networking and cooperation were realised. The rector discussed the novel challenges and solutions which university institutes were facing with the rise of the global knowledge economy:

> However, our surroundings for competition are in the process of changing rapidly. When previously, people left to study their degrees abroad only if they didn't receive a desired study place in Finland, nowadays we really have to compete in the supranational arenas for talented students and researchers as well as teachers. In addition, completely new agents are arriving in the field, for example different global distance and virtual universities. The new situation also challenges Finnish universities to search for network-based forms of collaboration outside of our country's borders. (The 1999 speech)

The themes concerning the rise of the global knowledge economy are discussed by the rector. The global competitive environment forces Finnish universities towards more dynamic and flexible procedures (per the 2002 speech). The European Union plays a role in the process of university reform in Finland. There are plans within the European Union to create a common research and teaching area (in higher education) in Europe (also per the 2002 speech). This is the way for Europe to develop as a competitive and knowledge-intensive continent (per the 2006 speech). The public discourse concerning globalisation and the effectiveness of Finnish universities accelerated during the beginning of the new millennium.

At the national level, there was a common public view that procedures were needed at universities for steering and reforming their management. The rise of the global knowledge economy (Hölttä, 1995; Pinheiro et al., 2016) is identified within the rector's discourse. The universities in Finland are expected to support social and economic development:

> ... the current Finnish university model, which is characterised not only by public funding, but also a relatively homogenous university concept – that is more clearly based on the idea of a knowledge-offering university than in many other countries. (The 2008 speech)

This case study fits into the grand discourses of the day, such as 'the organisation was shaped in order to compete in a global market economy' (Alvesson & Karreman, 2000, p. 1127), as the rector is pondering the cooperation:

> ... the motive is above all to respond together to the intensifying external competitive situation. (The 2007 speech)

A major university reform in Finland was accomplished in 2010. As a reflection to the international- and national-level change forces, the rector discusses in 2006 'The structures dominate the contemporary Finnish higher education policy discourse'. The structures refer mainly to the management and locational structures of Finnish higher education (per the 2006 speech). The general assumption behind the higher education structure discourse is 'the achieved benefits of the accumulation' (also per the 2006 speech).

As early as in 2000, the direction for the bigger university entities was discussed by the rector, as he introduced the concept of 'glocalisation'. The university operates in an environment which is global and local at the same time, as illustrated in Figure 2. The simultaneous processes of globalisation and localisation change the operational environment of the university organisation.

> A university similar to Joensuu, and not a larger one either, cannot throw oneself alone into this world. We must search for companionships both with other high education institutions and with companies, which again calls for a completely new operating culture and control models. In a world of infinite high education, universities are no longer under the nation-state's protection but are instead more independent than before, yet at the same time, agents that are vulnerable to risks and whose operational environment is at the same time local and international. Thus the oncoming change demands more advanced control of both internalisation and localisation from universities. (The 2000 speech)

The changing operational environment and political pressures towards efficiency appear as the main driving forces for a merger. The rector's discourse contains the theme of aiming toward common value, to sustain the institution's status as a research university.

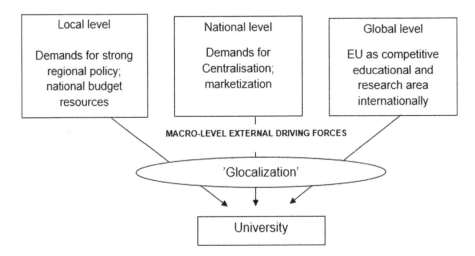

Figure 2. Macro-level external driving forces for change at different levels affecting the merger process of the two university organisations (Source: Karhapää, 2016, p. 137).

> … the predominant direction of change is the marketising and globalisation of the university institution. It seems that high education is governed by the viewpoints of customership and employment as well as intensifying supranational competition for good and paying students. Also in research, there is a notably growing pressure for commercialisation, which is followed by a strong specialisation in economically useful fields and bias in applications. As the missions of universities become differentiated, increasingly many of them are directed in a market-led way and only the "top universities" can afford to be truly 'universities of knowledge'. (The 2008 speech)

The act of merging aimed at common value (Lewis & Weigert, 1985) of being a competitive international research university. Thus, there seems to be a basis for trust to develop as the common value serves to bond the two university organisations.

The rectors of the merging universities, as the boundary spanners, are the key individuals (McEvily & Zaheer, 2006; Schilke & Cook, 2013; Vanneste, 2016) at the beginning of a new collaboration during the negotiation and planning processes (Ring & Van de Ven, 1994) of the 'new' university. Based on an interview in 2014 of the focal university's rector, the rector discusses how the personal chemistry between the two rectors was favourable from the focal university rector's perspective, a situation which seemed to push for the merger process. Despite the different scientific backgrounds, the communication between the rectors of the former university organisations was healthy (per the 2014 interview), which plays a key role in the development of interpersonal trust at the individual level (Fulmer & Gelfand, 2012). Thus, the further 'leap of faith' builds on the positive interaction and communication between the top managers. There were bases for trust to evolve and become part of the elements of the organisational-level actions.

Trust permeation at the group level – working groups as boundary spanners

In May 2007, the university boards of Joensuu and Kuopio approved the project plan for the 'new' university (Tirronen, 2008; Tirronen, Aula, & Aarrevaara, 2016). The commitment (Ring & Van de Ven, 1994) was made. There is diversity of views and interests, therefore strategic decisions will rarely be popular with all the parties concerned (Korsgaard et al.,

1995). Even though there was a positive interaction between the two rectors during the negotiation process (Ring & Van de Ven, 1994) at the individual level, the next administrative level met with suspicions between two university organisations during the commitment process (per the 2014 interview). The anxiety in the case university caused by the university reform and a merger of the two universities is perceived in the rector's discourse with reassuring words in 2007:

> This autumn, in the role of rector I do not think I can avoid those questions about the ongoing structural development of universities as institutions and the reform of the Universities Act – for us especially, the forming of a merged university in Eastern Finland - that is rising in Joensuu. If we shall succeed in their realisation, I believe that the whole scientific community in Joensuu will benefit from it without all of you having to grieve day and night because of the reforms. (The 2007 speech)

The rector's discourse recognises the two major changes, a merger and a university reform, facing the case organisation at once. The discourse emphasises that the aim of the merger is to reduce uncertainty and vulnerability by gaining knowledge and resources critical of the case university to survive in the long run (Klein, Palmer, & Conn, 2000):

> In principle, I consider it good that we can carry out these two – ... – changes at once. I am convinced that the change in juridical position would have compelled us to move forward with structural development without even starting the project of a merger university, but perhaps the alternatives would have then been more restricted. (The 2007 speech)

Interdependencies with the partner organisation begin to develop, bringing out the re-examination of the trustworthiness of the partner organisation (Schilke & Cook, 2013). Even though the merging universities have geographical similarity at the national level, there are cultural differences at the regional level: 'As we all know, up until now the regional boundaries in Eastern Finland have not been the easiest ones to cross' (from the 2012 speech).

In the commitment stage (Ring & Van de Ven, 1994) of a merger, the partner universities pursue an agreement on the strategy and structure for the 'new' university. Therefore, the university boards of Joensuu and Kuopio nominated a project management and 20 internal working groups at the Universities of Kuopio and Joensuu in May 2007. The management group consisted of two rectors and two directors of administration of the universities in Kuopio and Joensuu, and the vice-rector of the University of Joensuu. The 20 internal working groups were responsible for the actual planning work of the collaboration (Tirronen, 2008; Tirronen et al., 2016). By working together within these internal planning groups, more knowledge is gathered at the group level (Lewicki & Bunker, 1996) due to working role interaction (Ring & Van de Ven, 1994). Thus, based on repetitive interaction and communication, the gathered knowledge in addition to the rector's discourse suspends the suspicions, enabling the further 'leaps of faith' (Möllering, 2006) at the group level in the merging universities.

The merger was actualised in the commitment stage (Ring & Van de Ven, 1994) when the boards of the former universities decided the operational faculty structure of the 'new' organisation on 16 April 2008: '... (the strategy of the "new" organisation) entails focusing, which we can expect to occur this autumn when we decide the new faculties with the inner structures' (from the 2008 speech). Thirteen faculties of the partner universities merged into four big faculties of the 'new' organisation.

During the planning process of the merger in 2007, the rector discusses the formation of the 'new' organisation entity (per the 2007 speech). The motive for the merger was to develop one operational entity so that the basis of the different scientific cultures in the university and the geographical distance would be complementary and in opposition. If this was successful, the 'leap of faith' (Möllering, 2006) would be worth the risk. The competitiveness of the 'new' organisation would depend on the success of uniting the two universities as one operational and functional entity.

The 'leap of faith' and risk is present in the rector's discourse in 2014 when the rector recalls the merger process in 2008. There were suspicions and predictions concerning the intentions of the new partner during the strategy process in 2008:

> The strategy of the 'new' university is not to be implemented and turn into actions if the principles in the strategy are not jointly consented within a 'new' university community. Even though the strategy process during the merger (in 2008) was planned comprehensively with the new colleagues, there was still a suspicious atmosphere. The hidden and 'real' intentions of the new partner and colleagues were targets of speculation. Instead, during the planning process of the new strategy, I have perceived the whole new sense of communality. (The speech 2014)

There was quite a strong resistance to change at the middle administration level (per the 2014 interview). The reasons for the change resistance may be found among the main scientific fields and the administration cultures in the partner organisations (also per the 2014 interview). Medicine, as a primary scientific field, dominates in the University of Kuopio. On the other hand, the humanities (education and social sciences) are the major scientific fields at the University of Joensuu. Thus, the cooperation entails crossing the scientific borders between natural and human sciences. At the commitment stage of the inter-organisational relationship (Ring & Van de Ven, 1994), communication is one of the key mechanisms to build trust. The rector was discursively mitigating anxiety in 2007:

> I believe that in Joensuu and in Kuopio – in part together, in part separately- it has been possible to create such research prerequisites in a few top fields so that they are not only among the strongest research clusters in Finland but also among the well-known research clusters on a global level. (The 2007 speech)

Furthermore, the administration cultures were different in partner universities. The administration was centralised and built up around the medical discipline in Kuopio, whereas in Joensuu the administration was decentralised. The rector perceives that there was less need for discussions or meetings in the decentralised model of the faculty-centred administration in Joensuu. The administration culture was more self-directing in the Joensuu unit (per the 2014 interview). On the other hand, the Kuopio unit had a culture of discussing in committees and meetings, so to say 'dwelling on' administration (per the 2014 interview). This may be one reason for the cultural differences between administrations in the former university organisations (also per the 2014 interview). The merging universities have the history and routines of their own, yet they are to create and formulate the common routines and shared communication of the 'new' organisation:

> Many a discusser has fairly warned that the sole combining of administrative constructions does not guarantee academic excellence. That is why while developing structures, we should clearly separate those functions of the university where a larger size of unit really is beneficial and protects those good practices that have been birthed on campuses. (The 2007 speech)

When uniting two culturally differing organisations, the diversity of views and interests occur and may not be matched. Were these cultural differences too difficult to handle, some administrators 'remained there on the outer periphery' of the organisation in both of the former university organisations (per the 2014 interview). Most of the key administrators and other personnel who were unable to adjust to the change left the organisation (also per the 2014 interview).

The micro-level internal driving force for 'the leap of faith' and the formation of the new entity may be found among a new generation within the merging university organisations. The key position holders of the former organisations are to be replaced by younger ones. The younger generation in the university is used to cooperating and operating at a national and international level (Nevala, 2009). The preconceptions are fading away and new options and possibilities are recognised in the 'new' organisation after the merger. Thus, the intra-organisational element of a new generation serves as an important inter-organisational trust antecedent.

At the commitment stage of a merger, communication (Ring & Van de Ven, 1994) and information sharing are key mechanisms to build trust. The development of the new organisational processes based on fair and equal practices (Ring & Van de Ven, 1994) creates the basis for the cooperation between the members in the 'new' university. When the members of the partner universities interact directly based on their roles (Ring & Van de Ven, 1994; Vanneste, 2016) with one another at the group level, performing as boundary spanners and gaining more knowledge (Lewicki & Bunker, 1996), they are able to predict the behaviour of the other party, which builds trust. Trust that is established in relationships between the certain employees within the planning groups of the partner universities may permeate in intra-organisational trust at the organisational level (Schilke & Cook, 2013; Vanneste, 2016). These boundary banners may foster trust to permeate into the 'new' university reflecting the collectively held trust orientation between the members of the 'new' university (McEvily & Zaheer, 2006).

Trust permeation at the organisational level – execution of the merger

The execution of the merger on 1 January 2010 brings the commitments and rules of action into effect (Ring & Van de Ven, 1994). The case organisation is undergoing a dramatic change as the 'new' university organisation started operations towards uniting two equal, but culturally differing, universities. The rector eases the change anxiety by assuring discursively that it is the nature of the university institute: 'The dialectics of continuity and regeneration are characteristic of the whole university's essence' (the 2011 speech).

The novel and common practices are to be adapted. The routine and the domain of the ability of the employees changed. Some employees may experience shifts in status; at times, they also need to learn new ways of doing things. The rector manifests benevolence discursively:

> … we all should much more often thank our subordinates and why not also our colleagues for their important contribution for our mutual future. On my part I can express this gratitude here and now, also and especially for you who have openly and fairly expressed views that differ from the administration's policies in the midst of this change process. Where would criticism expressed in forward-looking spirits be seen as a driving force if not in universities? (The 2010 speech)

Synergies gained by the merger imply job losses; trust may be perceived to wither in a 'new' university organisation. The rector shows an interactive gesture towards employees with respectful words:

> My own feelings are quite divided amidst all this change. On the one hand, I am genuinely concerned for the stamina of the university staff, especially in a university like ours which merges on a profound level but also on a larger scale in the whole Finnish university institution. On the other hand, I can only admire the expertise and commitment that the members of our university community have shown during this fast-paced period of change. (The 2010 speech)

The geographical distance challenges the communication and interaction between the members in the 'new' organisation. The face-to-face interaction is costly (Bachmann & Inkpen, 2011) because the campuses are located 135 km apart. Therefore, knowledge-based trust formation (Lewicki & Bunker, 1996) is critical in the unifying university. The knowledge brings familiarity among the members between the partner universities and enhances trust (Gulati, 1995). As a result, e-communication could be utilised between campuses. The rector may build trust by offering general elements of interaction within the 'new' university organisation. By working together, colleagues will get to know each other beyond campus barriers; 'after the first contact and familiarisation, remote access functions as a natural communication platform' (from the 2010 speech). The effectiveness of communication benefits the 'new' university.

The trust development process is supported by the organisation-specific attributes (Schilke & Cook, 2013; Zucker, 1986) in a merging university. These organisation-specific attributes are to be identified among the national-level factors. There is a geographical similarity because of the location in Eastern Finland at a national level between the two merging universities. They also share a common establishment history in 1966 as a part of regional policy in Finland. Thus, the similar geographic location and organisational age support the positive trust assessments (Schilke & Cook, 2013) at the organisational level.

The common goal of being an international research university supports the trust development process in a 'new' university. Research, on the other hand, gains from the complementary disciplines of both of the partner universities. Larger scientific entities are possible; therefore, better opportunities for top international-level research exist. These industrial factors (Schilke & Cook, 2013; Zucker, 1986) can be interpreted in a way that creates safety and confidence in, and the positive expectations concerning, the ability of the 'new' organisation within the members of two university organisations. The common goal is manifested in the rector's discursive practice supporting trust to permeate in a 'new' organisation:

> The University of Eastern Finland has chosen the development towards a strong, multidisciplinary and international research university as the basic offset for the merging process. We are on the right track also according to rankings independent of us: today, the QS World University Ranking, one of the most essential global rankings, was published. According to it, the University of Eastern Finland ranked 308 among the universities of the world while we have set an ambitious goal for year 2015 to be in the top 200. (The 2010 speech)

Post-merger integration process: vision of identification-based trust

The formulation of a collective identity with shared values and the creation of the joint goals enhance identification-based trust (Lewicki & Bunker, 1996; Schilke & Cook, 2013) to develop after a merger. There are shared intra-organisational organisation-specific attributes within the merging universities which are important inter-organisational trust antecedents, such as similar organisational geographical location and age, younger generation, common aim and values. These may serve as additional driving forces for 'leaps of faith' and trust development within the 'new' organisation.

The rector promotes positive perceptions of a trusting state of mind for the future by advocating the goal of the 'new' university and its management. As being bigger and professionally managed, the 'new' university will meet the future challenges better than the two former organisations by themselves. Additionally, 'the voice of the larger organisation is heard with a more sensitive ear' (the 2010 speech).

The trust-building process is enhanced by creating novel organisational rituals. The rector is building 'the world in common' for the 'new' organisation by introducing common organisational rituals and procedures. There are new traditions included in the semester's opening ceremony which are meant to become permanent. There is a novel campus festival after the ceremony with a new sound of music – jazz. '… it is important for us, every now and then, to shake out our old routines' (the 2011 speech). The rector promoted the novel sense of community within the 'new' organisation by declaring that it has been one of the main priorities in management. The operational, managerial and physical structures of the new organisation are to be harmonised and integrated (the 2011 speech).

The rector builds trust (per the 2011 speech) by creating shared understanding of a common history of being multidisciplinary.

> Both of our predecessor universities had a multidisciplinary tradition in many ways. In Kuopio it meant that the whole university focused on interdisciplinary themes in health and the environment. In Joensuu, the multidisciplinary nature was linked to the ethical values of the university, if anything, but it was more concretely presented in ensembles broader than one study subject, such as research in education, border studies, colour research or environment studies. (The 2011 speech)

A vision to the 'new' university is given in the speeches of 2012 and 2014, which may be interpreted to enhance the identification-based trust development (Lewicki & Bunker, 1996). The rector emphasises the role of the employees as follows: 'Even though there is a great deal to be done with the structures of the "new" organisation, from now on, we have to take special care of the competitiveness of the academic core and good atmosphere in our university' (the 2012 speech). Two years later in 2014, the rector highlights the strategy of the 'new' university: '… key points are related, first, to more active recruitment and career policy of faculty members, second, to focusing our research on strong multidisciplinary research areas, and third, to developing educational programmes which meet the needs of tomorrow's working life'. By directing towards the common aim of being a competitive international research university, the mutual bond serves as a basis for the two organisations becoming one.

It is important to formulate a collective identity for the trusting parties. The launching of a visual image and the brand identity of the new organisation at the beginning of 2015 can be seen as an identification-based trust-building act, which will be enhanced by novel symbols of the rector soon.

The campus-specific 'flame' has been sustained in the emblems of the predecessor universities worn by us rectors. At the beginning of next year, the rector will wear a new necklace and robes designed for the University of Eastern Finland. (The 2014 speech)

Campus location is not the basis for the division of labour between the new rector and vice-rector from 2015 onward. The top management is reorganised with a view to uniting the new university. The aim is that campus barriers fade away, bonding the university as one entity. The vision of two organisations becoming one is signalled by the top management.

Summary and conclusions

This paper examines and reveals the multi-level dynamics of trust development as a top-down process where trust is based on calculation, knowledge and identification (Lewicki & Bunker, 1996) in association with the stages of negotiation, commitment and execution (Ring & Van de Ven, 1994) in a merger. Trust development processes and dynamics as the 'leap of faith' (Möllering, 2006) are studied in cooperative inter- and intra-organisational relationships at the individual, group and organisational levels. The empirical study is based on the qualitative longitudinal data of the rector's speeches analysed by a discourse analytical approach. The macro and micro perspectives of the merger are combined in this case study, with the source being at the individual level, from which the upper-management, group- and employee-level relationships are inferred.

The findings suggest that the macro-level external driving forces, such as the rise of the global knowledge economy, international competition and marketisation have direct effects on the organisation under study '... nowadays we really have to compete in supranational arenas for talented students and researchers as well as teachers' (discourse in 1999). The external driving forces enhance the calculation of the future benefits of the inter-organisational cooperation in order to cope with the changes. The rector expects more benefits gained than losses suffered from the future action of a merger 'as far as there are benefits achieved which are obvious for all the parties' (discourse in 2005). The macro-level external driving forces shape the micro-level organisational processes and relationships '... to respond together to the intensifying external competitive situation' (discourse in 2007).

The mutual aim of being an international research university serves bonding with partner universities enhancing the willingness to accept vulnerability at the organisational level during negotiation of a merger '... possible to create such research prerequisites in a few top fields so that they are not only among the strongest research clusters in Finland but also among the well-known research clusters on a global level' (discourse in 2007). The organisation-specific attributes (Bachmann & Inkpen, 2011; Schilke & Cook, 2013; Zucker, 1986), such as the similarity of industry, similar geographical location in Eastern Finland at the national level, similar organisational age, younger generation within the partner universities, common aim and values, suspend the uncertainties enhancing the willingness to accept vulnerability at the organisational level boosting 'the leap of faith' (Möllering, 2006). Moreover, it seems that the good communication and personal chemistry between the rectors of the partner universities at the individual level favour the cooperation, based on the interview in 2014 when the focal university's rector commemorates the merger process retrospectively.

Despite the good communication between the two rectors during the negotiation stage (Ring & Van de Ven, 1994) at the individual level, there are suspicions between the partner universities during the commitment stage (Ring & Van de Ven, 1994) '… in the role of rector I do not think I can avoid those questions about … the forming of a merged university … ' (discourse in 2007). A major change generates uncertainty, insecurity and vulnerability in the merging universities since the cooperation entails crossing the regional borders in Eastern Finland, and crossing the scientific boundaries of natural and human sciences, as well as meeting the cultural differences. The rector's discourse manifests trust do develop during the process '… , I believe that the whole scientific community … will benefit from it (merger) without all of you having to grieve … because of the reforms' (discourse in 2007), ' I am convinced that the change … would have compelled us to move forward with structural development without even starting … a merger' (discourse in 2007).

The partner universities pursue an agreement on implementing the merger in the commitment stage (Ring & Van de Ven, 1994) and nominate the internal working groups. The opportunities to gain more knowledge of the other partner during the repeated interactions within the planning group members at the group level may decrease suspicions, vulnerability and fear of opportunistic behaviour. The predictability of the behaviour of the other partner increases based on the increasing amount of knowledge '… there was still a suspicious atmosphere. The hidden and "real" intentions of the new partner and colleagues were targets of speculation (in 2008). Instead, … I have perceived the whole new sense of communality (in 2014)' (discourse in 2014). Thus, it seems that these prior interactions at the individual and group levels radiate to the members of the 'new' university supporting trust to develop at the organisational level.

The novel common organisational rituals and traditions promote a sense of community within the 'new' university in the execution of a merger. The rector's discourse may build a collective identity with shared values and practices 'Both of our predecessor universities had a multidisciplinary tradition' (discourse in 2011), as well as support continuous interaction in order to sustain ongoing relationships '… we should clearly separate those functions of the university where a larger size of unit really is beneficial and protect those good practices that have been birthed on campuses' (discourse in 2007).

The rector's discourse manifest the trust development act by developing positive expectations and common goals '… the University of Eastern Finland ranked 308 among the universities of the world while we have set an ambitious goal … to be in the top 200' (discourse in 2010), '… more active recruitment and career policy of faculty members, … , to focusing our research on strong multidisciplinary research areas' (discourse in 2014). The discourse of the rector spreads throughout the merging university promoting interaction '… we all should more often thank … our colleagues for their important contribution for our mutual future' (discourse in 2010). Top management signal the aim of campus barriers fading away, bonding the university as one entity by adjusting the duties of the rector and the vice-rector in a way that the campus location is not the basis for the division of labour.

When trust develops in the 'new' university, the communication is more effective. This is especially important due to the long geographical distance between the partner universities. The e-communication is cost-effective and supports the competitiveness expectations and practices of the 'new' university '… after the first contact and familiarisation, remote access functions as a natural communication platform' (discourse in 2010).

There is a need to interact, such as to complete the negotiation-commitment-execution cycles, continuously in a 'new' university to reason the terms of the organisational relationships.

Inevitably, the situations arise when the terms of the relationship need to be re-thought and negotiated, especially as the cooperation entails crossing the scientific and the campus barriers. Therefore, the continuous interaction is needed in the 'new' university in order to sustain the relationships. Active management is called for to build cooperative relationships in a 'new' university by deliberately promoting interaction because through a series of working role interactions, the parties concerned also become more familiar with one another personally at an individual level. This may increase interpersonal trust, as opposed to inter-(working) role relationships. Over the course of time, these interactions provide grounds for identification-based trust to grow, especially when the continuous interaction is supported by fair and equal organisational processes. Consequently, the ongoing relationships and intended benefits of the action of a merger may be preserved.

Limitations, future directions and implications

This study is conducted as a qualitative intensive single-case study in order to bring as much understanding and interpretation as possible from one case. The social reality is constructed subjectively and is based upon perceptions and experiences which might appear differently for each person. The social reality is context-specific and might change over the course of time (Berger & Luckmann, 1972). It needs to be noted that the researchers are a part of the organisation under study. The involvement in the organisation might unintentionally affect this study. To perform as an insider within the case organisation and simultaneously examine it as an outsider might result in some limitations in the study. However, involvement also brings insights and novel perspectives to the contextual case. The researchers have a deep tacit understanding and engagement with the case organisation that may enhance the depth of the interpretive case study. The ability to understand the field and the context of this case study assists the credibility (Eriksson & Kovalainen, 2008) of the results of the research. The researchers have been aware and avoided bias while doing this research. Moreover, besides the case organisation, the researchers have periodically worked away from the case organisation and in other organisations, which has allowed multiple perspectives on the case organisation. The preliminary research report was sent to read to two actors concerning this study (the rector and an administrator) for comments. This assists the conformability (Eriksson & Kovalainen, 2008) of the study.

This study concentrates primarily on the top management perspective that leaves avenues for future research. It would be fruitful to extend the exploration of trust development processes from other perspectives in the merging organisation. Further research may extend to studying the views of employees and students in the merger. Finally, the role of trust in the post-merger integration process needs further exploration and may involve the views of the merger-veterans as well as the 'newcomers'.

When two organisations merge, the organisational benefits such as enhanced competitiveness and effectiveness for a larger organisation are expected. There is a possibility that the expected and intended benefits of the merger may not be realised. The most challenging stage of the merger is to integrate the two organisations into becoming one (Fubini et al., 2007; Pinheiro et al., 2016; Vaara & Tienari, 2002). This study produces empirical knowledge on how trust emerges and permeates through the inter- and intra-organisational relationships at multiple levels in a merger context. By focusing on the discourse of the rector, i.e. how 'the words' influence and how the discourse over the course of 17 years builds rationale behind the organisational strategic actions and supports the trust development process during a merger. The study also recognises and provides elements for the management of the post-merger integration process by emphasising the importance of continuous interaction supplemented by efficient and equal organisational practices.

The findings imply to practising managers that the management exerts influence through discourse, by which trust may be built in organisations. Through interaction, trust may form a potential intangible asset (Savolainen, 2011; Savolainen & Lopez-Fresno, 2013) evolving a resource that unifies the merging organisation.

Disclosure statement

No potential conflict of interest was reported by the authors.

References

Aldrich, H., & Herker, D. (1977). Boundary spanning roles and organization structure. *Academy of Management Review, 2*(2), 217–230.

Alvesson, M., & Karreman, D. (2000). Varieties of discourse: On the study of organizations through discourse analysis. *Human Relations, 53*, 1125–1149.

Bachmann, R., & Inkpen, C. (2011). Understanding institutional-based trust building processes in inter-organizational relationships. *Organization Studies, 32*, 281–301.

Berger, P. & Luckmann, T. (1972). *The social construction of reality. A treatise in the sociology of knowledge*. Harmondsworth: Penguin Books Ltd.

Boon, S. D., & Holmes, J. G. (1991). The dynamics of interpersonal trust: Resolving uncertainty in the face of risk. In R. A. Hinde & J. Groebel (Eds.), *Cooperation and prosocial behaviour* (pp. 190–211). Cambridge, UK: Cambridge University Press.

Burr, V. (2003). *Social constructionism* (3rd ed.). London: Routledge.

Cameron, E., & Green, M. (2004). *Making sense of change management. A complete guide to the methods, tools & techniques of organisational change*. London: Kogan Page Limited.

Cartwright, S., & Cooper, C. (1990). The impact of mergers and acquisitions on people at work: Existing research and issues. *British Journal of Management, 1*, 65–76.

Clark, R. B. (2004). *Sustaining change in universities*. Berkshire: Open University Press, McGraww-Hill Education.

Currall, S. C., & Inkpen, A. C. (2002). A multilevel approach to trust in joint ventures. *Journal of International Business Studies, 33*, 479–495.

Demers, C. (2007). *Organizational change theories. A synthesis*. Los Angeles, CA: Sage.

Eriksson, P., & Kovalainen, A. (2008). *Qualitative methods in business research*. London: Sage.

Fairclough, N. (1992). *Discourse and social change*. Cambridge: Polity Press.

Fubini, D., Price, C., & Zollo, M. (2007). *Mergers: Leadership, performance & corporate health*. New York: Palgrave MacMillan.

Fulmer, C. A., & Gelfand, M. J. (2012). At what level (and in whom) we trust: Trust across multiple organizational levels. *Journal of Management, 38*, 1167–1230.

Giddens, A. (1990). *The consequences of modernity*. Stanford: Stanford University Press.

Gulati, R. (1995). Does familiarity breed trust? The implications of repeated ties for contractual choice in alliances. *Academy of Management Journal, 38*, 85–112.

Hölttä, S. (1995). *Towards the self-regulative university*. University of Joensuu Publications in Social Sciences, 23, Joensuu.

Karhapää, S.-J. (2016). *Management change and trust development process in the transformation of a university organisation*. Publications of the University of Eastern Finland. 122. http://epublications. uef.fi/pub/urn_isbn_978-952-61-2174-1/

Kaukonen, E., & Välimaa, J. (2010). Yliopistopolitiikan ja rakenteellisen kehittämisen taustoja [Backgrounds of university politics and structural development]. In H. Aittola & L. Marttila (Eds.), *RAKE - Yliopistojen rakenteellinen kehittäminen, akateemiset yhteisöt ja muutos [RAKE- Structural development of universities, academic communities and change]*, Final report of RAKE – project 2008–2009, 13-20. Opetusministeriön julkaisuja 2010:5 (Publications of the Ministry of Education 2010:5). Helsinki, Finland: Opetusministeriö (Ministry of Education).

Klein, K. J., Palmer, S. L., & Conn, A. B. (2000). Interorganizational relationships: A multilevel perspective. In K. J. Klein & S. W. J. Kozlowski (Eds.), *Multilevel theory, research and methods in organizations: Foundations, extensions, and new directions* (pp. 267–307). San Francisco, CA: Jossey-Bass.

Korsgaard, A. M., Schweiger, M. D., & Sapienza, J. H. (1995). Building commitment, attachment, and trust in strategic decision-making teams: The role of procedural justice. *Academy of Management Journal, 38*, 60–84.

Kozlowski, S. W. J., & Klein, K. J. (2000). A multilevel approach to theory and research in organizations: Contextual, temporal and emergent processes. In K. J. Klein & S. W. J. Kozlowski (Eds.), *Multilevel theory, research and methods in organizations: Foundations, extensions, and new directions* (pp. 3–90). San Francisco, CA: Jossey-Bass.

Langley, A., Smallman, C., Tsoukas, H., & Van de Ven, H. A. (2013). Process studies of change in organization and management: Unveiling temporality, activity and flow. *Academy of Management Journal, 56*, 1–13.

Lewicki, J. R., & Bunker, B. B. (1996). Developing and maintaining trust in work relationships. In R. Kramer & T. Tyler (Eds.), *Trust in organizations* (pp. 114–139). Thousand Oaks: Sage.

Lewis, J. D., & Weigert, A. (1985). Trust as a social reality. *Social Forces, 63*, 967–985.

Mayer, C. R., Davis, H. J., & Schoorman, D. F. (1995). An integrative model of organizational trust. *Academy of Management Review, 20*, 709–734.

McEvily, B., & Zaheer, A. (2006). Does trust still matter? Research on the role of trust in inter-organizational exchange. In R. Bachmann & A, Zaheer (Eds.), *A handbook of trust research*. (pp. 280–300). Surrey, GBR: Edward Elgar.

MinEdu. (2015). The Bologna Process. The Finnish Ministry of Education and Culture. Retrieved from http://www.minedu.fi/OPM/Koulutus/yliopistokoulutus/yliopistot/?lang=en

Minzberg, H. (1973). *The nature of managerial work*. New York, NY: Harper & Row.

Minzberg, H. (1983). *Structure in fives: Designing effective organisations*. Prentice Hall, NJ: Prentice-Hall.

Möllering, G. (2001). The nature of trust: From Georg Simmel to a theory of expectation, interpretation and suspension. *Sociology, 35*, 403–420.

Möllering, G. (2006). *Trust: Reason, routine, reflexivity*. Oxford, UK: Elsevier.

Möllering, G. (2013). Process view of trusting and crises. In R. Bachmann & A. Zaheer (Eds.), *Handbook of advances in trust research* (pp. 285–305). Cheltenham: Edward Elgar.

Möllering, G., Bachmann, R., & Lee, S. H. (2004). Introduction: Understanding organizational trust – Foundations, constellations, and issues of operationalisation. *Journal of Managerial Psychology, 19,* 556–570.

Nevala, A. (2009). *Uudisraivaaja. Joensuun yliopiston 40-vuotis historia [Pioneer. The 40-year history of University of Joensuu].* Saarijärvi: Saarijärven Offset Oy.

Nooteboom, B. (2002). *Trust. Forms, foundations, functions, failures and figures.* Cheltenham: Edward Elgar.

Perrone, V., Zaheer, A., & McEvily, B. (2003). Free to be trusted? Organizational constraints on trust in boundary spanners. *Organization Science, 14*(4), 422–439.

Phillips, N., & Hardy, C. (2002). *Discourse analysis.* Thousand Oaks, CA: SAGE.

Pinheiro, R., Geschwind, L., & Aarrevaara, T. (2016). A world full of mergers: The Nordic countries in a global context. In R. Pinheiro, L. Geschwind, & T. Aarrevaara (Eds.), *Mergers in higher education. The experience from Northern Europe* (pp. 3–28). Switzerland: Springer.

Riad, S. (2005). The power of 'organisational culture' as a discursive formation in merger integration. *Organization Studies, 26,* 1529–1554.

Ring, S. P., & Van de Ven, H. A. (1994). Developmental processes of cooperative interorganizational relationships. *Academy of Management Review, 19,* 90–118.

Savolainen, T. (2011). Leadership by trust in renewing intellectual capital. In A. Puusa & H. Reijonen (Eds.), *Aineeton pääoma organisaation voimavarana [Intangible capital as an organizational resource]* (pp. 117–141). Kuopio: UNIPress.

Savolainen, T., & Ikonen, M. (2016). Process dynamics of trust development: Exploring and illustrating emergence in the team context. In S. Jagd & L. Fuglsang (Eds.), *Trust, organizations and social interaction: Studying trust as process within and between organizations* (pp. 231–256). Cheltenham: Edward Elgar.

Savolainen, T., Lopez-Fresno, P., & Ikonen, M. (2014). Trust-communication dyad in inter-personal workplace relationships – Dynamics of trust deterioration and breach. *The Electronic Journal of Knowledge Management, 12*(4), 232–240. Retrieved from at www.ejkm.com

Savolainen, T., & Lopez-Fresno, P. (2013). Trust as intangible asset – Enabling intellectual capital development by leadership for vitality and innovativenes. *The Electronic Journal of Knowledge Management, 11*(3), 244–255. Retrieved from at www.ejkm.com

Schilke, O., & Cook, S. K. (2013). A cross-level process theory of trust development in interorganizational relationships. *Strategic Organization, 11,* 281–303.

Schoorman, D. F., Mayer, C. R., & Davis J. H. (2007). An integrative model of organizational trust: Past, present, and future. *Academy of Management Review, 32,* 344–354.

Searle, H. R., & Ball, S. K. (2004). The development of trust and distrust in a merger. *Journal of Managerial Psychology, 19,* 708–721.

Stahl, G., Mendenhall, M., Pablo, A., & Javidan, M. (2005). Sociocultural integration in mergers and acquisitions. In G. Stahl & S. Sitkin (Eds.), *Mergers and acquisitions managing culture and human resources* (pp. 3–16). Stanford, CA: Stanford University Press.

Stahl, G., & Sitkin, S. (2005). Trust in mergers and acquisitions. In G. Stahl & S. Sitkin (Eds.), *Mergers and acquisitions managing culture and human resources* (pp. 82–102). Stanford, CA: Stanford University Press.

Sydow, J. (2006). How can systems trust systems? A structuration perspective on trust-building in inter-organizational relations. In R. Bahmann & A. Zaheer (Eds.), *A handbook of trust research* (pp. 377–392). Cheltenham: Edward Elgar.

Tirronen, J. (2008). *Itä-Suomen yliopistohankkeen prosessiarviointi 1 [The process evaluation of the formation of the University of Eastern Finland 1].* Kuopio: Kuopion yliopisto (University of Kuopio).

Tirronen, J., Aula, H.-M., & Aarrevaara, T. (2016). A complex and messy merger: The road to university of eastern Finland. In R. Pinheiro, L. Geschwind, & T. Aarrevaara (Eds.), *Mergers in higher education. The experience from Northern Europe* (pp. 179–193). Switzerland: Springer.

Vaara, E., & Tienari, J. (2002). Justification, legitimization and naturalization of mergers and acquisitions: A critical discourse analysis of media texts. *Organisation Studies, 9,* 275–304.

van Dijk, A. T. (2001). Critical discourse analysis. In D. Schiffrin, D. Tannen, & H. E. Hamilton (Eds.), *The handbook of discourse analysis* (pp. 352–371). Chichester: Blackwell.

Vanneste, S. B. (2016). From interpersonal to interorganisational trust: The role of indirect reciprocity. *Journal of Trust Research, 6,* 7–36.

Vihko, R. (2007). *Itä-Suomen yliopisto – tulevaisuuden yliopisto ajassa [University of Eastern Finland – The university of the future in contemporary era]. Opetusministeriön työryhmämuistioita ja selvityksiä 2007:15.* Helsinki: Ministry of Education.

Vuorio, K. (2006). *Lentoon. Kuopion yliopiston neljä vuosikymmentä [Take-off. The four decades of University of Kuopio].* Saarijärvi: Offset.

Yin, K. R. (2003). *Case study research: Design and methods.* Thousand Oaks, CA: Sage.

Zucker, G. L. (1986). Production of trust: Institutional sources of economic structure, 1980-1920. In M. B. Staw & L. L. Cummings (Eds.), *Research in organizational behavior: An annual series of analytical essays and critical reviews* (pp. 53–111). Greenwich, CT: Jai Press.

Appendices

Appendix 1. Data: speeches as texts

Year	Title of the speech	Number of Words	Pages
1998	JOENSUUN YLIOPISTON PAIKKA INFORMAATIO – JA GLOBAALITALOUDESSA (The Position of University of Joensuu in Information and Global Economy)	1631	6
1999	KUUMA SYKSY (Hot Autumn)	1901	7
2000	SUOMALAINEN YLIOPISTOMALLI JA RAJATTOMAN KORKEAKOULUTUKSEN HAASTEET (The Finnish University Model and the Challenges of Borderless Higher Education)	1933	6
2001	ALUEELLINEN YLIOPISTOPOLITIIKKA – YLIMITOITETTUJA ODOTUKSIA JA NIUKKOJA VÄLINEITÄ (The Regional University Politics – Oversized Expectations and Scarce Resources)	2000	7
2002	KANSALLINEN YLIOPISTOLAITOS TIENHAARASSA (National University Institute in its Crossroads)	1816	7
2003	YLIOPISTO ON ENEMMÄN KUIN OPPILAITOS (University is more than A School)	1814	7
2004	JOENSUUN YLIOPISTO KANSAINVÄLISTYMISEN JA ALUEELLISTUMISEN RISTIAALLOKOSSA (The University of Joensuu between Internationalisation and Regionalisation)	1779	9
2005	KUMOUS VAI REFORMI (Revolution of Reform)	1975	5
2006	RAKENTEELLISEN KEHITTÄMISEN SYVÄRAKENTEITA (The Metastructures of Structural Development)	1996	9
2007	LIITTOYLIOPISTON HAASTEET (The Challenges of a Federal University)	2072	7
2008	HUOMISEN YLIOPISTO (The University of Tomorrow)	1671	6
2009	40 VUOTTA JOENSUUN YLIOPISTOA: MUUTOKSIA JA JATKUMOITA (Forty Years of the University of Joensuu: Changes and Continuities)	1485	5
2010	YHDESSÄ ETEENPÄIN (Together Forward)	1477	6
2011	SIVISTYSYLIOPISTO AJASSA (The Civilisation University Today)	2116	6
2012	SUOMEN LAAJA-ALAISIN TIEDEYLIOPISTO ITÄ-SUOMESSA (The most Multi-Field University in Eastern Finland)	1506	5
2013	KOULUTUS JA OPISKELIJAT OVAT OLENNAINEN OSA TIEDEYLIOPISTOA (Education and Students are an Essintial Part of a Science University)	1808	5
2014	UUDET ASKELMERKIT (New Steps)	1681	7
TOTAL		30,661	111

Appendix 2. Interview

The interview with the rector 19 November 2014 at 14:15–16:00 hrs at Rector's office, Aurora II-building, 3rd floor, Joensuu campus, University of Eastern Finland

I Organisational Change and University Management

What kind of change was it to start as a rector; how did you see and feel the shift from the professorship to rectorship in 1998?

How was the first period of your rectorship; what special things do you remember during the period 1998-2002?

On what basis and how did the merger decision emerge from 2003-2007?

What kind of process, from your perspective, were the reform of the university organisation and the merger of two university organisations?

What challenges were there in the merger of University of Joensuu and University of Kuopio? What challenges are there for the future?

What procedures are important at the final stage of the merger process once the situation and changes are stabilised?

II The University annual semester opening ceremony speeches of the rector

How do you prepare the annual semester opening ceremony speeches?

Where do you get the impulses for the content of the speeches? (What are the channels through which you inject issues into speeches?)

How do you see/hear/sense the impact of the speech?

What special issues that the speech has raised in conversation do you remember?

What channels do you receive feedback from concerning the speeches, especially concerning the feedback, reactions and thoughts of the university organisation and the staff?

To whom are you directing the speech (who are you thinking of when you prepare the speech?)

How do the speeches come about (preparation process/themes/content)?

What feelings do the speeches raise in (you) the rector?

III The rector as a manager in university

What kinds of key moments of management have you experienced during your career; when has there been a clear need to manage?

How well did you know the University of Kuopio and the people there?

What kinds of challenges have you faced (experienced) concerning communication and inter-action during the merger process with the members of University of Kuopio and similarly with the University of Joensuu (negotiation and communication)?

Where does the power of the university rector originate from, what are sources of the power and where and how does the power arise?

How has the decision making of the university rector been transformed after the university reform of 2010?

How has the role of the university board changed in university management?

How has the role of the ministry of education changed in university management or governance (during your rectorship)?

Contextualising the coevolution of (dis)trust and control – a longitudinal case study of a public market

Lena Högberg ⑩, Birgitta Sköld ⑩ and Malin Tillmar ⑩

ABSTRACT
Research into the dynamics of trust–control is still inconclusive. In this paper, we offer an in-depth understanding of how (dis)trust and control coevolve as embedded in multiple dimensions of context. The paper focuses on public markets, a context which is underrepresented in extant studies on trust and control. Our analysis is based on a longitudinal case study of interorganisational relationships (IOR) between boundary spanners representing purchaser and providers on a customer choice market for home care in a midsized municipality in Sweden. We identify, narrate and analyse critical incidents during seven years of the process. A conceptual framework contextualising the trust–control nexus of a public–private IOR is developed and utilised. We find that while the public–private IOR context requires control, control only enables deterrence trust from the municipal officers and only in individual providers. Interferential rather than symbiotic coevolution of trust and control is the dominating pattern. In addition, we find what we denote as *mixed coevolution*, where control simultaneously has positive and negative impact on trust. In our case in point, control enables trust in specific providers but this trust is not reciprocated due to experienced distrust on the category level.

Introduction

The trust and control nexus has been the subject of a lively academic discussion (cf. Bijlsma-Frankema & Costa, 2005; Costa & Biljsma-Frankema, 2007; Six, 2013). Research results are inconclusive and empirical studies with a dynamic process perspective have been called for (Costa & Biljsma-Frankema, 2007). Bradach and Eccles (1989) viewed price, authority and trust as three control mechanisms that are both substitutable and complementary. Since then, some researchers have argued that control tends to undermine trust (Neu, 1991), others that control and trust are substitutable (Fukuyama, 1996), and yet others that control mechanisms may enhance trust (Sitkin, 1995; Sztompka, 1999). Numerous theoretical papers (i.e. Choudhury, 2008; Das & Teng, 1998, 2001; Ferrin, Bligh, & Kohles, 2007; Inkpen & Currall, 2004; Six, 2013; Vlaar, Van den Bosch, & Volberda, 2007; Weibel, 2007) on trust and control have offered propositions on the relationship as well as discussed how previous studies can be integrated and reconciled. To mention a few studies: the nexus has been analysed in relation to various forms of control and trust (Das & Teng, 2001), the initial conditions of trust (Vlaar et al., 2007), and how and in what form control is developed and executed (Weibel, 2007). It has also been argued that the trust–control nexus depends on the wider embedding context (Edelenbos & Eshuis, 2012; Tillmar & Lindkvist, 2007).

Trust in public sector arrangements is vital for a democratic society (Choudhury, 2008; Goodsell, 2006; Kim, 2005; Oomsels & Bouckaert, 2017), but public contexts are underrepresented in the field of trust research (Edelenbos & Klijn, 2007; Six, 2013). Within public administration, the need for what is called trust-based governance has been enacted and is currently increasingly emphasised (Edelenbos & Klijn, 2007; Vallentin & Thygesen, 2017). This also applies to Sweden, where the government has appointed a 'trust commission' to shed light on and evaluate pilot cases of trust-based governance (Bringselius, 2017). The focus is on intraorganisational trust. However, during the past decades New Public Management (NPM) reforms have increased the number of interorganisational relationships (IOR) in the public setting (Edelenbos & Klijn, 2007; Hodge & Greve, 2007). The IORs take forms such as public–private partnerships, cross-sectoral cooperation or networks, and are regarded as complex and challenging (Bryson, Crosby, & Middleton Stone, 2006; 2015). Public markets comprise a large portion of the economy: 16 per cent of Gross Domestic Product in the European Union alone (the European Commission, 2017). Scholars have concluded that trust across borders is both more difficult (Child, 1998) and more important (Li, 2012), but such research, particularly concerning sectoral borders, is still scarce. Hence, in line with Brown, Potoski, and Van Slyke (2007), we argue that the context of public–private IORs is particularly interesting for an exploration of the interplay between trust and control.

The objective of this research is to examine the role and dynamics of trust and control between boundary spanners in a public–private interorganisational relationship. The paper reports from a longitudinal case study of a customer choice market for home care in a midsized Swedish municipality. It contributes with insights into how (dis)trust and control coevolve over time across levels of analysis, exploring how the process is impacted by context in general and the customer choice model in particular. Since boundary spanners have been found to play a crucial role in the process of trust in interorganisational relationships due to their direct interaction with one another (Oomsels & Bouckaert, 2017; Vanneste, 2016) we pinpoint the perspectives of boundary spanners of both the public and the private parties of the interorganisational relationships.

The paper is structured as follows. A conceptual framework is developed in relation to theory and a review of previous research on the dynamics of trust–control in the specific context of public markets, suggesting a contextualisation approach. The framework is followed by a description of the methods employed in the empirical research project and analysis. The case description and analysis is followed by a discussion in which we discuss our findings in relation to the framework. The paper ends with conclusions and implications as well as suggestions for further research.

Analytical framework

We define trust itself in accordance with the seminal paper by Rousseau, Sitkin, Burt, and Camerer (1998, p. 395) as 'a psychological state comprising the intention to accept vulnerability based upon positive expectations of the intentions or behaviour of another'. The emergence of trust, or distrust, is a continuous dynamic process (Oomsels & Bouckaert, 2017) linked to what is perceived as 'good reasons' for trust (Lewis & Weigert, 1985). Nonetheless, trust always requires a leap of faith (Möllering, 2001). 'Good reasons' for trust (Rousseau et al., 1998) include *deterrence trust* where trust is based on the existence of control, *calculus trust* based on credible information, and *relational trust* when emotions are added to the state of trust. During the evolution of trust between *specific* actors, they assess each other's trustworthiness in terms of their *ability* (competence trust) and *intentions* (goodwill trust) (Nooteboom, 1996). However, trust is a multilevel phenomenon also affected by our preconceptions of different *categories* of people (Tillmar, 2005; Zucker, 1986).

Control is here defined as 'a regulatory process by which the elements of a system are made more predictable through the establishment of standards in the pursuit of some desired object or state' (Das & Teng, 2001, p. 258). Das and Teng (2001) distinguish between *behavioural control* (ensuring appropriate process), *output control* (assessing members' performance) and *social control* (shared values, beliefs and goals) and propose that both output and behavioural control have negative effects on trust, whereas social control has positive effects. Control may be one of the perceived 'good reasons' (Lewis & Weigert, 1985) for trust, as it affects a person's possibilities to act opportunistically (cf. Rousseau et al., 1998).

Extant literature provides contradictory interpretations of the trust–control nexus. Costa and Biljsma-Frankema (2007) distinguish between (1) the substitution view, (2) the complementary view and (3) the contextual-based view. The substitution view (1) assumes that high trust enables low control and that low trust necessitates high control (cf. Williamson, 1975; Gambetta, 1988), but argue that there is a lack of empirical evidence for that (Costa & Biljsma-Frankema, 2007). The complementary view (2) holds that both trust and control contribute to cooperation and that they can reinforce each other. For example, laws and regulations provide a predictability which enables cooperation and development of trust (cf. Luhmann, 1979; Tillmar, 2006; Zucker, 1986). Vlaar et al. (2007) discuss how IORs can develop into vicious or virtuous circles in relation to trust and control. Within the contextual-based view (3), as explained by Costa and Biljsma-Frankema (2007), the nexus depends on the type of control used (Das & Teng, 2001). The relationship has, however, also been found to be dependent on the institutional context (Deakin & Wilkinson, 1998; Rus & Iglic, 2005; Tillmar & Lindkvist, 2007).

We argue that these inconclusive research results call for an analysis of the specific contextual dimensions involved, in order to better understand the interplay (Möllering, 2005) and coevolution (Edelenbos & Eshuis, 2012).

Previous research on trust–control dynamics in public sector contexts

In public management, the scholarly interest in the subject of trust is increasing (Argento & Peda, 2015; Getha-Taylor, 2012; Oomsels & Bouckaert, 2014) but given the context of the public sector's legal, social and regulatory systems, control is always involved to some extent (Edelenbos & Eshuis, 2012; Six, 2013; Vadelius, 2015; Vallentin & Thygesen, 2017).

Based on a literature review of research published in 1990–2017 (summarised in Appendix 1), we can conclude that only a limited number of papers shed light on trust–control dynamics in public IORs. We find that the previous studies on trust–control in IORs display a pattern somewhat similar to that recognised by Costa and Biljsma-Frankema (2007). In arguing for a shift from control focus to trust focus, both Huque (2005) and Singh and Prakash (2010) lean towards seeing the phenomena as substitutable. Some papers take an interest in how not only control, but also trust, can be *used* by the public organisation as a complement to control the behaviour of service providers (Chen, 2009; Ditillo, Liguori, Sicilia, & Steccolini, 2015), or a creative sector where quality is not easily measured (ter Bogt & Tillema, 2016). Trust is found to complement regulations and price when public purchasers choose providers for their care markets (Mannion & Smith, 1998).

In contrast to Costa and Biljsma-Frankema (2007), we find that most previous studies show that the trust–control nexus depends on a broad spectrum of contextual issues. For instance, Argento and Peda (2015) argue that the relationship between trust and contract is contingent on the mode of informality and frequency of interaction between the contracting parties. Cäker and Siverbo (2011) argue that control is affected by type of trust, but that trust can be unaffected by control. Milbourne and Cushman (2013) demonstrate how trust in public agencies is eroded among third sector providers due to use of competitive markets, control and lack of communication.

Taken together, previous research shows the importance of a contextual approach. By context we generally mean the 'situational opportunities and constraints that affect behavior' (Johns, 2006, p. 386). The following section is denoted, based on theory and the results of the literature review, to develop a contextual approach to guide the analysis of trust–control dynamics in public–private IORs.

A contextualisation approach to trust–control in public–private IORs

As a basis for contextualising the interplay of trust–control we propose targeting the broader dimensions of context introduced by Johns (2006) and developed by Welter (2011), who discusses context as comprised of *business* (industry, market); *social* (network, household, family); *spatial* (geographical environment, community) and *institutional* (culture, political and economic system) context.

On public markets, or quasi-markets (Ferlie, Ashburner, Fitzgerald, & Pettigrew, 1996), both public and private organisations provide publicly funded services that are free of charge to the users of the services. When analysing public markets it is of particular importance to understand the particularities of the public sector (Kastberg, 2005; Norén, 2003; Yttermyr, 2013). The variety of actors involved in this kind of market increases the complexity of the interorganisational relationships (Tillmar, 2009). Public markets are organised differently depending on local prerequisites and ways of translating ideas (Blomqvist & Rothstein, 2000).

The customer choice system is a voucher system which enables the customer to choose a provider, thus giving the customer a larger degree of power (Le Grand, 1991). In a customer choice system, authorisation criteria are decided by the municipality and only providers who apply and fulfil the criteria are included in the system. These criteria can differ from one municipality to another, as can the model for distributing clients who are unable or unwilling to choose a provider (Högberg & Mitchell, 2015; Sundin & Tillmar, 2010). The key actors in a customer choice model are the *customers,* the service users who choose an authorised provider; the *providers*, all the organisations authorised to perform the care services; and the *purchaser*, the municipality, who is ultimately responsible for the services provided, for authorising providers and the party paying for the services (service users pay in relation to income and only a small fraction of the cost). The role of the municipality in a customer choice system is hence partly that of purchaser and partly that of an agent of the citizens (Berlin, 2006). All key actors contribute to and have impact on how the market is organised. The actors involved have their specific positions, motives and strategies that can be in conflict with other actors' interests, resulting in a dynamic organising process where there is always some uncertainty about the outcomes of the interplay (Ahrne, Aspers, & Brunsson, 2015).

The municipal organisation is multifunctional, governed by elected representatives and entitled to balance interests including the rule of law, control, transparency, openness, predictability and cost efficiency (Christensen, Laegreid, Roness, & Røvik, 2007). On customer choice markets, municipalities have the responsibility and power to organise the market to meet these challenging demands. As an organiser of the market they have the power to use a range of control elements to regulate the providers, such as deciding on who is involved in the market (authorisation of providers), rule-setting, monitoring procedures and sanctions.

The suppliers who engage as providers on public markets can be public, private or not-for-profit organisations. The interests of the small private providers targeted in this study are multiple too, albeit of different sorts as compared to public organisations, as they must balance the interests of all their primary stakeholders in order to be sustainable (Clarkson, 1995). There is typically strong interdependence between a private corporation and its shareholders, customers, suppliers and employees besides the governmental bodies that govern the sector. If any of those primary stakeholders were to withdraw from the corporate system, it would seriously damage the corporation (Clarkson, 1995).

Due to their direct interaction with one another, boundary spanners are of particular importance to comprehend the process of trust in IORs. It is the boundary spanners who, based on their interaction and subjective evaluation of previous experiences of one another, decide on whether or not the other party is trustworthy (Oomsels & Bouckaert, 2017). Vanneste (2016) argues that trust between organisations evolves through a bottom-up process, which starts with interpersonal trust that spreads to the organisational level and becomes interorganisational as a result of indirect reciprocity. As proposed by Schilke and Cook (2013), a common understanding within one organisation that another organisation is trustworthy may also trigger the development from individual-organisation trust to organisation-organisation trust. Longitudinal empirical studies capturing such processes are needed, argue Schilke and Cook (2013). Hence, the contextual embeddedness of public–private IORs is expected to influence the interplay of trust–control as boundary spanners are required to mind the specific prerequisites of the organisation they represent. In our case analysis, we aim to elaborate exactly *how* the contextual dimensions presented in this framework influence this interplay.

Given the public sector embeddedness of the IORs targeted, there is reason to consider Oomsels and Bouckaert's (2014) proposition that trust as well as distrust may be both *functional* and *dysfunctional* in public administration. Trust is *functional* when suspension of vulnerability enables goal orientated collaboration. However, too much trust may be *dysfunctional* and costly if the trustor becomes improvident. Distrust might be *functional*, albeit costly, through regulations serving to avoid vulnerability, or *dysfunctional*, when regulations and contracts constrain fruitful collaboration. Based on previous research

(Oomsels & Bouckaert, 2014), we can hence expect to find both functional and dysfunctional aspects of trust, as well as distrust, in the interplay of trust and control in this particular context. (Dis)trust between boundary spanners is to be understood as a state of mind that, at any point in time, can be placed on a continuum from distrust to trust (cf. Rousseau et al., 1998).

In the context of the public market, control is a behaviour directed only from the municipal organisation to the provider organisations. Based on extant literature (e.g. Das & Teng, 2001; Edelenbos & Eshuis, 2012), it is reasonable to assume that the type of control, as well as how forms of controls are utilised in the IOR, has an impact on the dynamics of trust and control in a public–private IOR. An analysis of the interplay of (dis)-trust–control should hence include the forms of controls and methods by which the municipality governs the behaviour of providers. Based on previous research (Das & Teng, 2001), we can expect that social control is less likely than behavioural and output control to have negative effects on trust.

Based on a literature review Vlaar et al. (2007) describe how IORs can develop into vicious or virtuous circles in relation to trust and control. Based on an empirical study Edelenbos and Eshuis (2012) suggest that trust and control coevolve with time in either symbiotic or interferential circles depending on whether control supports or undermines trust. With a focus on managerial control, Weibel (2007) proposes that the design process and implementation of control are of vital importance. A participatory development of the formal control and constructive feedback is proposed to have positive effects on value internalisation and trustworthiness while rewards and sanctions based on standards are proposed to have a negative effect. Given the asymmetry of the public and private organisations involved in IORs on public markets, the ways of introducing control might be of similar importance for the coevolution of trust–control as in Weibel's (2007) study.

Vlaar et al. (2007) argue that the level of (dis)trust in the initial stages of an IOR is important for understanding how the relationship will evolve as it impacts both control and IOR performance. The initial levels of trust and distrust have a strong influence on how controlling behaviour undertaken later on is interpreted. Similarly, Edelenbos and Eshuis (2012) argue that the initial relationship is of particular importance for the direction of the coevolution of trust–control into symbiotic or interferential patterns. On a related note, it has been demonstrated that behaviour undertaken to restore broken trust can be interpreted as distrust, hence having negative effects (Sitkin & Stickel, 1996; Vlaar et al., 2007).

Based on the above, we could also expect that in an IOR between a public authority (such as a municipality) and a subcontractor (such as an SME), a high degree of participation in design and implementation of control is conducive to virtuous circles of trust–control coevolution, while a non-participatory approach to control could be expected to have an opposite impact. Furthermore, we can expect that the initial levels of (dis)trust are of particular importance for the direction of this coevolution. Finally, we can expect that efforts to restore trust can be perceived as distrust and result in an interferential coevolution of distrust–control.

Method

Capturing the complex interplay of contextual dimensions of the trust–control nexus arguably calls for a qualitative case study approach as it enables us to generate a rich empirical description of the phenomenon (Yin, 2013) as embedded in context (Eisenhardt & Graebner, 2007). This paper builds on a longitudinal case study of a customer choice market for home care services in a Swedish municipality of midsize hereafter referred to as 'Fieldtown'. The case is of particular relevance for analysing trust–control as the local regulations offer the authorised providers substantial autonomy, hence putting matters of trust and control to the fore. The paper focuses on the years 2010–2017, a phase in which the number of small private providers first increased substantially, then decreased as a result of increased control and distrust.

Studying processes of trust and distrust empirically is challenging since it is theoretically a state of mind (Rousseau et al., 1998). What we can capture is but the materialisations of such states of mind, taking the form of actions and oral or written accounts. The paper is based on an interpretive organisational research approach (Prasad & Prasad, 2002), which means that we consider the process by which trust as well as control is socially constructed as boundary spanners involved in IORs share their interpretations of actions and experiences made.

Our empirical material consists primarily of interviews and documentation such as authorisation applications, agreements and decisions taken by the municipality during the process. Interviewees include representatives of the purchaser (municipal officers and politicians) and the providers (small business owner-managers and their deputies). Key interviewees, the boundary spanners, were interviewed on repeated occasions to form the longitudinal understanding necessary to fulfil the research objective. Interviews were in-depth and lasted about one and a half hour on average, focusing on the interviewee's lived experiences of either acting on the customer choice market (small private providers) or acting to organise the market (municipal officers).

To represent the perspective of small private providers, two boundary spanners were selected. Both 'Khabat' and 'Aminah' are small firm owner-managers engaging as providers in the Fieldtown customer choice market. They enter the market at different points in time and together their experiences make up a relevant variation of perspectives. Their counterparts, the boundary spanners of the municipal organisation, are the municipal officers responsible for carrying out the political decisions made by the elderly care services committee regarding authorisation of providers and controlling the quality of services delivered. The material is focused on the boundary spanners who have the most direct contact with providers, first 'Kristina' and 'Ulla', and subsequently 'Eva' and 'Margareta'.

We approached the material iteratively similar to the process described by Eisenhardt and Graebner (2007, p. 25) as 'recursive cycling among the case data, emerging theory, and later, extant literature'. We utilised the *critical incident technique* (CIT) (Münscher & Kühlmann, 2012) to identify critical factors in the process. The strength of the CIT method is arguably in collecting and analysing data that make visible the effects of certain behaviour on trust, including the creation, strengthening or destruction of trust (Münscher & Kühlmann, 2012). CIT was used to pinpoint situations where trust could be interpreted as either created, strengthened or diminished in relation to control efforts. By analysing how patterns of trust and control coevolve in the specific context we developed emergent theories that were then related to the findings of previous research.

A literature review was conducted systematically in the Scopus and Web of Science databases to explore the extent and specific topics covered concerning trust and control in the context of public sector interorganisational relationships as published in articles and book chapters 1990–2017. Key search terms include 'trust', 'control' and 'public'. Only articles discussing both trust *and* control (or contract as a type of control) were included. The 16 publications that met the criteria are outlined in Appendix 1.

Based on the literature review we conducted further readings of the critical incidents found in the case, looking for complementary or contrasting findings to those of previous research. Having found gaps in the previous literature, we developed a theoretical framework, making use of literature on trust–control in combination with theory of context (Johns, 2006; Welter, 2011) as well as theories of public sector organisation prerequisites (Christensen et al., 2007) and private company prerequisites (Clarkson, 1995). The framework provided a frame for further analysis as well as a means to explain the patterns found.

The case of Fieldtown

The case highlights critical incidents identified as important to the coevolution of (dis)-trust–control between municipal officers and small private providers in the Fieldtown customer choice market. Appendix 2 offers an overview of the process.

Marketisation reform has been continuous in Sweden since the 1980s, facilitated by new legislation including the Act on System of Choice in the Public Sector (2008:962). The principle of local autonomy (Local Government Act, 1991:900) means that elected representatives of the municipality decide on the ways in which services are to be provided. When introducing a customer choice market for home care services in Fieldtown, the right-wing majority of the elderly care services committee were seeking an organisational solution that would facilitate more options for care recipients by increasing the diversity among providers. The elderly care services committee (from now on *the committee*), comprising elected municipal politicians, is ultimately responsible for the care and services provided. In Fieldtown, providers who have the necessary qualification can apply for authorisation to conduct the assessment of the client's needs that is typically performed by the Social Services. This means that the provider has a greater responsibility in Fieldtown than elsewhere in Sweden. For political reasons, the criteria for authorisation were set to attract new providers. Providers who are authorised are not guaranteed any clients and it is up to each provider to attract clients. The municipal provider along with large companies had an initial advantage over small and new ones in the customer choice market as they were already established in Fieldtown and recognised as providers of elderly care. Amongst the few small private firms who gave the new market a go, it was soon realised that it was quite difficult for them to attract clients.

Khabat – first of the small providers

One of the entrepreneurs who took the step to seek authorisation to provide care is Khabat. Khabat was born in Iraq and speaks six languages. He had completed the upper secondary school nursing programme and had worked as a care assistant at a large company providing elderly care before starting Khabat Care. In his authorisation application he describes his firm as employing two relatives and tending to one (1) client in need of 225 hours of personal care per month.

The municipal officers of the elderly care services department (from now on *the department*) are responsible for enacting the authorisation procedure as well as for supporting and controlling the performance of providers. The assessment of Khabat's application states that Khabat does not meet the requirements regarding formal competence and experience. It is proposed by officers Kristina and Ulla, and decided by the committee in February 2011, that Khabat Care be authorised to provide a limited number of hours of home care (160 per month) but that all decisions regarding service users' needs must be made by the Social Services. Khabat is unhappy with the decision:

> They were a bit cautious at first even though I could demonstrate good references. … It was war between me and them, because I wanted to increase the number of hours that I could produce. They increased the level from 160 to something like 500. But I wanted to develop further.

As Khabat gains experience and can demonstrate satisfied clients he is allowed to produce more hours. However, reports repeatedly question how he reports hours produced, which causes suspicion among municipal officers. Khabat Care heavily exceeds the hours that the firm is authorised for, and provides care after 10 pm. Kristina and Ulla summon Khabat to a meeting in October 2011 for a reprimand. To prove his capability to the municipal authority, Khabat studies to gain further qualifications.

With time, Khabat's firm is allowed to produce more hours. In 2014, after some years of operation, Khabat's business has grown. The firm now has 41 service users and 31 employees. Khabat recruits a coordinator with the formal competencies required by the municipality, a university degree in the health care professions, and she brings knowledge on how to organise the operations in a professional manner. Once more Khabat applies for authorisation to perform needs assessments and again his application is rejected by the municipality. He has undergone the education required, yet is denied full authorisation since it is found that he himself, not the coordinator, is the actual manager. He describes the situation as one of mutual distrust, where mistakes for which he is held accountable (such as erroneous invoices) consistently turn out to be mistakes on the part of the municipality (such as miscommunication between Social Services and the department). The 'war' with the municipality thus continues.

The municipal officers' dilemma

In the light of the committee's objective to increase the number of small providers, the establishment of firms like Khabat Care is positive. However, the inexperience of new small providers causes the officers some concern. Eva explains:

> As municipal officers we are torn in two here, … as we have this political objective stating that the number of small firms with less than ten employees must increase. We have to work for that goal. On the other hand, we want the companies who are included in the care system to be able to do the job, so that the clients aren't harmed. This certainly isn't easy.

The dilemma concerns the lack of competence demonstrated by the new firms when delivering home care, both in terms of care and in terms of management:

> We have spent disproportionate amounts of time and resources to help them. We did not presume them to be business people and fully-fledged managers but it is very difficult when we cannot send them a form to fill out.

To reinforce the requirements for management competence, the municipal officers propose a revision of the specification criteria for authorisation, including the contract with the providers who are already authorised. Various education efforts are offered. The differences in support needs between large and small providers causes the officers to hold separate meetings for small and large providers. The large organisations are represented by middle managers with the same professional qualifications as the municipal officers of the department, thus speaking the same language, as Eva describes it. The small providers have completely different queries. A further dilemma is that the officers in the department do not themselves have the sufficient competence to educate or even understand the small firm owner-managers. The officers are typically educated professionals in nursing or social work, not business management.

If a provider is found not to comply with the criteria in the 18-page contract, the officers respond with patience and information, Eva argues. The reason is that diversity is key for the customer choice system to actually offer more freedom of choice for the clients. She explains:

> We know the political significance of this freedom-of-choice motive and that in a customer choice market we must treat all the providers equally, and here you can obviously see that we don't. If [one of the large firms] were to say something like that [they can't take on only one client in a remote area due to the impact on profitability even though they have applied to provide in that area], then there would be no excuse. No, it is the freedom of choice, the diversity perspective, which has won over the contract.

The 'limited needs assessment' procedure is unique for Fieldtown and increases the municipal officers' dilemma as it calls for a trustworthy party, who will not take advantage of the opportunity and allow the client more hours than necessary in order for their own firm to make a profit. According to Eva this procedure poses an obstacle to the inclusion of small providers. A procedure by which the providers only perform the care decided upon by the Social Services would facilitate the inclusion of small providers, implying that the officers trust the small providers to perform the care but not to conduct the needs assessment. Khabat is a case in point in this dilemma. His clients are satisfied and have no reason to complain. 'In that respect it seems to work', Eva says, and adds that the concern regards the significant volumes of hours produced as well as Khabat's competence. 'He is very frustrated with us', she concludes. Small providers who offer both home care and personal assistance services are the most difficult to deal with, according to Eva.

> It is very important to state that it is not our view that they cheat intentionally. That is not what we are saying. Rather, they lack the knowledge, they don't understand the differences.

Aminah – the former municipal employee

In early fall of 2014 yet another provider with competencies in several languages, Small Town Care, receives authorisation. The owner-manager, Aminah, is a qualified nursing assistant who was previously employed for 18 years by the municipal care provider as a nursing assistant. Unlike several other small firms, Small Town Care offers only home care, with no parallel services such as personal assistance. Aminah was encouraged to start her own firm by a former manager who thought that Aminah had both the knowledge and experience of care work as well as the language competences and the drive to do the job. Aminah's authorisation is approved within just two weeks of submitting her application.

A new control programme

In September 2014 the local government elections result in a power shift in the municipality. After eight years of rule by the right-wing alliance the municipality is to be governed by a coalition of Social Democrats, Greens and Liberals. With the new political majority, the objectives for the department are altered to focus more on the quality of services produced than on who performs them. Having a large number of small providers offering diversity of services is no longer an end in itself.

Officers at the department voice criticism of the current provision of home care. Since the introduction of the customer choice system, there has been no general control effort. A quality control programme is decided on by the committee and implemented by the department from June 2015. Politicians and municipal officers agree on the importance of a review that is broad in its scope and includes all providers, not only the private ones, as they do not want to signal distrust in them in particular. One of the committee members, Anna, specifically mentions that trust between the municipality and the private providers is important, as 'Fieldtown has a long history of close dialogue between the parties [the municipality and private companies].' She concludes that the 'reliable' providers are happy with the quality control, since it is a means for them to demonstrate that they do a good job. Anna states that it is important to control providers in order to make sure that any opportunistic behaviour is prevented and that fine examples of good services are highlighted.

The quality control programme targets areas including the organisation of operations, staff education levels, and actual hours spent with clients in relation to billing. Different accounts are compared, such as needs assessment and staff schedules, salary reports and financial reports.

Municipal officers too argue that the control effort reinforces and ensures that the trust they put in providers is legitimate. Eva states that providers who are found to perform needs assessments that are out of proportion, such as allowing three hours for taking a shower, lose the municipality's trust as a consequence. Her colleague, Margareta, who is one of the officers responsible for the review, agrees and adds:

> In such cases, the trust that the provider has in both helping the client and applying for the help, but also in terms of setting the limits to the service, this trust is then eaten into.

Where minor deviations are found, the providers and municipal officers engage in dialogue to construct an action plan for each provider to deal with the deviations. Almost all the private providers reviewed, including one of the large providers, are followed up in a subsequent review regarding financial aspects. A midsized firm, with a general profile and no language niche, is the first to be excluded from the customer choice system as a result of the control effort, due to significant deviations from the contract. Municipal officers, including Eva and Margareta, express relief that this firm is not one of the niched small providers who offer home care in a foreign language. Municipal officers agree that it is very important to keep the companies in the language niche operating as they meet a need in the market. The hard part is making them act according to the contract, they conclude.

Providers are excluded as a result of the new control programme

The quality review of Khabat Care is performed in several steps. Khabat brings his lawyer, a consultant and his operations manager to the first meeting with Margareta and the other municipal officers performing the review. The review finds that Khabat Care is still not formally qualified to perform the limited needs assessment and that the criteria in the contract are not being met. Criticism is also directed at the committee for authorising Khabat's Care in the first place. By the subsequent review, Khabat has had some months to implement necessary revisions but fails to do so and the contract is subsequently terminated.

Khabat is annoyed with the decision to withdraw his authorisation. His firm has done everything to comply with the rules and norms, he argues. He has consulted former managers in established provider organisations to ensure the firm's organisational routines and claims that hours are reported in a correct manner. His interpretation of the situation is that the municipal officers distrust him based on his status as an 'immigrant' and argues that 'They don't want to see an immigrant succeed.' Khabat takes the case to court, but loses.

Aminah and her firm comes out well from the quality review process. In March 2016, when the review is conducted, the company employs six staff, including the owner-manager, and provides home care services to 14 clients. Aminah herself is the only qualified nursing assistant but the organisation is in the process of recruiting. The records state that the firm meets the quality criteria on all accounts. In addition, even though Aminah is trained and authorised to conduct a limited needs assessment, the company has only engaged clients via the Social Services.

By late 2016 when the quality control programme is finalised, seven firms have seen their contracts terminated due to non-compliance with the criteria or breach of contract. The reasons include inaccurate financial reporting and violation of working laws. The officers conclude that the original criteria were set too low and that this has made it possible for non-trustworthy companies to enter the market. Margareta states:

> We need to set the requirements higher from the beginning in order not to include any irresponsible companies. Because that is what this comes down to, non-competent management. … That they don't understand the business they are in.

The main error, according to Margareta, is the quality management of the small firms:

> They did not understand the importance of having a quality management system, what it must include, how to get the staff involved and understand the system.

Working conditions are also given increased importance. The ratio between staff working hours and compensation awarded has been found not to be in line with either social services or employment legislation. Margareta draws the conclusion that the private providers pay too much attention to the 'business aspects'. There are even cases where the officers have found reasons to report providers to the police for fraud, where providers have received compensation from the municipality on incorrect grounds.

A higher threshold and increased controls

In March 2017 a new authorisation specification is decided upon by the committee to make sure that the providers meet the municipality standards. The new criteria stem from experiences made in the quality reviews and include clarifications regarding quality assurance system and measures to ensure client safety and good work conditions for staff. Formal education at university level in a relevant profession such as nursing or social work is now a requirement for the acting manager, or 'demonstrated competence' in equivalence to this. This is, according to municipal officers, to make sure that competent providers such as Aminah are not excluded from providing services.

In addition, yet a new control system is implemented to continuously follow up on the providers. 'We will track the providers much more closely now than before', Margareta says, adding that 'If they start out on the wrong path then hopefully we will discover that much sooner and can correct them.' As a result, Margareta says, they now have more trust in the providers who remain in the system.

Among the remaining providers is Aminah and Small Town Care who by now provides home care to 47 clients and employs 32 persons. Although still in business, Aminah's view is that the municipality does not want small private providers, that they are not trusted to do the job well. She interprets the quality reviews as a means for the municipality to shut them out:

> They review us 200% more than they do the large providers. … Every day there is something new that they want to look up and investigate. What's next? What will be the next point of control?

The constant reviews leave Aminah with a sense of frustration and discrimination. The reviews are also time-consuming. To make sure her firm fulfils the requirements, Aminah has employed a deputy manager who is both a qualified nursing assistant and holds a university degree in social work. She has experience of working with several organisations, including Social Services. The vision Aminah holds for the future includes neither expansion nor diversification, but simply a stable local organisation specialising in home care to elderly clients with foreign backgrounds. Even though her firm passed the control measures she is not confident that she has gained the trust of the municipality. Aminah and her deputy manager both describe a situation in which small firms with owner-managers of foreign background are being treated in a discriminatory way by the municipality and the large providers. Aminah has the impression that politicians, municipal officers and managers of the larger organisations distrust them. Her deputy adds that even a small sense of trust from the municipalities would make a big difference to the providers, who try their best:

> When you feel that you follow the rules and you know the law and do everything you are told but still hear 'You did not behave, what have you done?', then how can you do a good job? I wish that there was at least 20% trust in the small providers. Then things would have been fine. Then they would not have had to – and I am not saying that all small providers have behaved properly 100% and maybe that is what is causing the suspicion with the others – but they lump everyone together. That's how it feels!

Aminah's sense of a lack of trust in her and in other small providers is a cause for constant concern and worry:

> We will see if we are allowed to continue. … There is that constant worry regarding the municipality. You never know what they will do next. We struggle on and work and keep the clients satisfied. … The municipality keeps talking about caring for the client but still we don't always know what it is that they want. You never know if you are meeting the criteria of the contract.

Despite the uncertainty, Aminah and her deputy are determined to carry on and do what they think is meaningful and right for the client. They follow the rules as best they can, making adjustments where necessary. 'We will put up a fight, we will show them it can be done', Aminah concludes.

Discussion

Having described the coevolution of (dis)trust–control empirically by pinpointing critical incidents in the case of Fieldtown, we now discuss the results in the vocabulary of the analytical framework.

(Dis)trust–control dynamics as embedded in context

As expected based on the analytical framework we find that the contextual embedded-ness influences the interplay of trust–control in the case of Fieldtown, as the boundary spanners mind the prerequisites of their particular organisations when interacting.

The longitudinal approach enables us to consider the *time context*, tracking the evol-ution of (dis)trust–control as a process. This process is influenced by developments not only on the local level, but also by national and international trends (Pollitt & Bouckaert, 2011). In Sweden, as in many other countries, marketisation has been continuous since the 1980s (Erlandsson, Storm, Strads, Szebehely, & Trydegård, 2013). New Swedish legis-lation for public procurement (Public Procurement Act 'LOU', 1992:1528/2007:1091) in general and customer choice systems (Act on System of Choice in the Public Sector 'LOV', 2008:962) in particular has facilitated the process. On a local level, the customer choice reform as such, as well as the priority of supporting small scale private providers, is understood as politically motivated at a certain point in time. As times and political climate change, priorities change, and hence also the prerequisites for trust and control in the eyes of the officers, as is clear from the case study.

A key feature of public markets is the *institutional context*, which is of importance to comprehend the prerequisites of the boundary spanners representing different organis-ations and why they are faced with different 'rules of the game' depending on these roles. Elderly care is the responsibility of the municipality but as the Social Services Act (1980:620) regulates only the services as such, and as the 290 municipalities in Sweden are autonomous (Local Government Act, 1991:900), each municipality can design their public markets to fit the preconditions of the local society. Simultaneously, the officers have multiple interests to handle besides the rule of law, including control, transparency, openness, predictability and cost efficiency (Christensen et al., 2007). Given these prerequi-sites, complete trust in small private providers in general is arguably dysfunctional if there is limited basis to assess goodwill and/or competence, and some degree of distrust is hence functional. For example, trusting a business manager without an education in a care profession to make the limited needs assessments to determine the home help hours that the business he owns will earn, as in the case of Khabat, would not have been appropriate given the institutional context of the IOR. The municipal officers' distrust in Khabat which necessitated the control (that in turn led to deterrence trust) can hence be interpreted as functional. The political system is another aspect of institutional context (Welter, 2011) that influences the prerequisites for trust on behalf of the municipal officers acting as boundary spanners. In the initial phase, Eva and her colleagues are required by political objectives to facilitate for private providers in relation to an interpretation of the authorisation criteria that causes issues of trust in terms of provider competence. In a second phase, political mandates and priorities change into a focus on controls to make sure that all authorised providers are trustworthy both in terms of competence and in terms of goodwill. We hence find that what is deemed as functional trust in the eyes of one political mandate is deemed dysfunctional in the eyes of another, altering the prerequisites for trust between boundary spanners.

With the private providers, a number of stakeholders' demands must be met in order for the business to be able to continue (cf. Clarkson, 1995). If the demands are in conflict, the provider must either prioritise one interest over the other or find a way to make them meet. As the customer choice market model does not guarantee the providers any clients, the clients that have chosen a certain provider gain a position of power with that provider. Aminah and Khabat both focus on a certain niche of clients based on language and culture, and see it as their competitive advantage to meet the demands of these specific clients. The result is a potential conflict of interest with the demands of the municipal authority, as discussed in more detail in the next section. In the eyes of the municipality, Aminah manages to balance the demands of both clients and the municipality better than Khabat. As a result, Aminah is trusted whereas Khabat is deemed to act opportunistically and hence distrusted.

The above is closely linked to the *business context*, which concerns the market dimensions (Welter, 2011). As the market is regulated by one of the organisations in the IOR, there is a strong asymmetry in the relationship. The market for home care in Fieldtown was relatively new when Khabat applied for authorisation. Yet at that time large providers had already established themselves as legitimate in the eyes of municipal officers. The small firm was a new category for the municipal officers to grasp, and there was no pre-existing category-based trust. Hence, the specific trust in firm owners was especially important. Adding to the difficulty for small new firms was the local Fieldtown procedure of limited needs assessment, calling for an even more trustworthy party than in other customer choice systems. The market constitution and the dominance of large providers render the small firm providers a weak negotiation position. The small business dependence on the municipality makes the relationship more vertical than horizontal. Hence, this particular context makes the IOR asymmetrical, affecting the coevolution of trust–control to a high extent.

The *spatial context* refers to the circumstances of the local community (Welter, 2011), here Fieldtown in Sweden. Fieldtown is a midsized municipality where there are enough elderly in need of home care to sustain a market of several providers in terms of volume, local variations and submarkets. Fieldtown also has a large enough number of citizens who request home care in languages other than Swedish, which opens up for the niche in which both Khabat and Aminah find legitimacy for their businesses. Yet Fieldtown is not a big city, and the distance from one end of town to another is short. In terms of trust, interaction between purchaser and providers is enabled by the close proximity of offices, enabling frequent meetings, but hampered by the lack of opportunity for spontaneous and informal contact that a co-localisation would enable. In a purchaser–provider system, too close a personal and informal contact between boundary spanners would not be deemed appropriate for reasons of competition, and hence it is not suggested as a solution but rather a complicating factor in terms of trust.

The *social context* dimension is perhaps the one causing most problems in the Fieldtown process of trust–control, in terms of social categorisations. Khabat and Aminah are both operating in an ethnic niche of the market, providing home care in languages other than Swedish. They are also both of non-Swedish origin. From previous trust research (Tillmar, 2005; Zucker, 1986) we know that social categories matter with regard to who is perceived as trustworthy. Although the boundary spanners representing the municipal elderly care services department never articulate such a stance, both Khabat and Aminah perceive their behaviour as a sign of category-based distrust related to ethnicity. This triggers vicious circles of distrust–control.

The role of unidirectional control

Our case study reveals that control has a profound impact on trust, contrary to some previous research such as the case described by Cäker and Siverbo (2011). What we see in Fieldtown is at first a lack of small providers from the politicians' perspective. They want more diversity and freedom of choice, but fail to attract small providers due to constraints in the form of economies of scale. When small firms enter the market – the first of which is Khabat – and the municipal officers assess their trustworthiness they induce goodwill but not enough competence (cf. Nooteboom, 1996). Through a supportive and educational approach, the municipal officers strive to help Khabat develop enough competence to gain their trust. The piecemeal socially-oriented controls and interaction enable the municipal officers to place enough trust in his competence to take, if not a leap of faith (Möllering, 2001), at least a small *step* of faith (Tillmar & Lindkvist, 2007) involved in deterrence trust (Rousseau et al., 1998) to continue the contract. This supportive approach on behalf of municipal officers can also be explained based on the satisfaction demonstrated by Khabat's clients in his services, which gives the municipal officers incentives to continue the contract and serves as a basis for calculus-based trust.

It is our interpretation that the educational efforts of the municipal officers were vital to maintain the interorganisational relationship in the initial phases. The new quality control system introduced in 2015 was primarily based on behavioural and output control in the terms of Das and Teng (2001). Only the requirements related to profession and education can be regarded as a form of social control (Das & Teng, 2001), as profession and education often include a component of shared beliefs, values and goals. When the general approach, initiated by officers and decided by the new political majority of the committee, is changed, a vicious circle of control–distrust begins. In other terms, we witness interferential, coevolution of trust and control (cf. Edelenbos & Eshuis, 2012) in the case of Khabat after the changes in forms of control. The Fieldtown case hence supports previous research stating that social control is less likely to result in interferential coevolution of trust–control than behavioural and output controls.

Furthermore, it is our contention that the interferential coevolution has to do with *how* the change of control was introduced. The asymmetrical nature of the studied IORs makes them resemble a hierarchical management control situation. As Weibel (2007) argues, control systems should be designed in a participatory way and implemented in a non-standardised manner including constructive feedback, in order not to have negative effects on trust. The small business owners in Fieldtown perceived the controls to be neither participatory nor constructive. In this case, we have seen how a standardised top-down introduction of a new control system lead to vicious circles also in a public market IOR context.

Mixed coevolution of (dis)trust and control

In the case of Fieldtown, we find instances of both interferential and symbiotic coevolution of trust and control (Edelenbos & Eshuis, 2012) but also observe a third type of process, one which we label 'mixed coevolution'.

When, based on changing and increased control efforts in 2015, evidence of opportunistic behaviour on Khabat's part is found, the calculus-based trust developed is replaced by distrust. The officers assess their initial distrust as having been functional (cf. Oomsels & Bouckaert, 2014). After yet another try at establishing trust, Khabat loses his contract and authorisation in late 2016. Khabat experiences the distrust on behalf of the municipality to be based on an erroneous assessment and he in turn distrusts both the municipal organisation and individual municipal officers. This distrust is expressed when he takes the case to court. He loses, and the mutual distrust increases.

The increased control efforts lead to both *distrust in and from specific providers* and more controls to make sure that all who are not trustworthy are excluded. Yet, municipal officers argue, the controls also lead to increased *trust in specific providers* based on a combination of deterrence (Rousseau et al., 1998) and perceived ability of those who comply with contract criteria. In Aminah's case, the municipal officers start off with relational trust (Rousseau et al., 1998). She is known to them by association (having been employed by the municipal provider for many years) and is assessed as having the relevant practical experience in care to compensate for her lack of higher education. In such a situation, with high initial trust, others (Vlaar et al., 2007) have argued that virtuous circles are likely to occur. However, our case shows a more complex pattern. The municipal officers' view of developing trust in Aminah by means of control resembles a symbiotic process where control leads them to find reasons to trust Aminah as she continuously passes the tests that they present, both in terms of competence and goodwill. However, the experience of a symbiotic process is not reciprocal. Aminah's view is, to the contrary, that she is being controlled to a greater extent on the basis of being categorised as a 'small provider' and an 'immigrant', which is why she loses her trust in the municipality. For her, the process is interferential rather than symbiotic. Although Aminah comes out well in the controls, and officers perceive their trust to have been functional, she, like Khabat, perceives the treatment as unequal from that of large providers and that treatment of providers of a Swedish background differs from that of providers of a non-Swedish background. Our interpretation is that the two providers experience *category-based distrust* (Tillmar, 2005; Zucker, 1986), i.e. they experience that there is more distrust in providers of a non-Swedish background. By the municipal officers, Khabat is distrusted and Amina is trusted. However, both providers distrust not only the goodwill of the municipal boundary spanners but eventually the municipality in general.

The case demonstrates how virtuous circles of coevolution of trust–control can turn into vicious circles. Hence, the coevolution is not necessarily dependent on the initial stage, to the extent previously argued (Edelenbos & Eshuis, 2012; Vlaar et al., 2007). Based on our longitudinal case study, we argue that coevolution is, instead, continuously affected by contextual dimensions. Therefore we coin the term *mixed coevolution*. Mixed coevolution is at hand when both trust and distrust develop simultaneously as a result of control. For example, mixed coevolution can be a result of different impacts of control on the boundary spanners from the organisations involved in the IOR. Even if control has enabled the more powerful controlling partner to trust its counterpart, that trust is not necessarily reciprocated. When that is not the case, mixed coevolution also occurs. Furthermore, divergence in the (dis)trust directed towards *categories* of actors and *specific* counterparts within those categories, may also cause mixed coevolution.

From the above, we find reason to enrich the contextualisation framework with the term *mixed coevolution*, and modify the expectation that initial levels of trust determines the direction of the coevolution. Consistent with expectations from previous studies is, however, that efforts to restore trust can be perceived as distrust.

Contributions, implications and further studies

To date, empirical studies on the trust–control nexus within the field of trust research have largely focused on the private sector. The few existing studies of public markets are published in public administration and management journals (as demonstrated in Appendix 1). This paper contributes to the trust–control literature in the following ways:

- We have developed an analytical framework for the contextual interplay of trust and control when embedded in a public–private IOR setting.
- Findings from a longitudinal case study has been discussed in relation to expectations based on previous trust research in similar contexts to further the understanding of coevolution of (dis)trust and control in public–private IORs on public markets.
- We have demonstrated not only virtuous circles of symbiotic coevolution of trust and control, but also vicious circles of interferential coevolution (cf. Edelenbos & Eshuis, 2012). The boundary spanners' interactions, experiences and partly differing contextual embeddedness are found to be key to understanding the complexity.
- An important conclusion is that the coevolution can be simultaneously interferential and symbiotic, and we hence coined the term *mixed coevolution* to conceptualise such patterns.
- The mixed coevolution, we argue, can be understood as a consequence of diverging embeddedness of the IOR boundary spanners, and demonstrated in different levels of (dis)trust in specific individuals and in a category of actors.

Implications

From the case of Fieldtown, and in line with Chen (2009), we argue that the trust–control balance is delicate but vital for the functioning of public markets. Hence, this balance needs to be analysed in relation to market construction. Given that municipalities want to support diversity on public markets and encourage small scale service provision, the system needs to enable not only control but also possibilities to interact and develop mutual trust. While public markets require some degree of control, the kinds of control that are used and how forms of control are implemented can be directed in order to enable trust. Less direct monitoring and more socially orientated control seem preferable from a trust perspective, as does a participatory approach to developing and implementing control systems.

Further studies

The case study reported in this paper highlighted the dynamics of (dis)trust–control in a particular municipality in Sweden, with its particular prerequisites. A comparative approach to study the phenomenon of contextual embeddedness of (dis)trust–control would be a relevant path to further the analysis of the contextual factors influencing the nexus.

Other questions emerging from this study relate to the impact of category-based trust. Does trust presuppose homogeneity between organisations? If so, of what kind? The organisations involved in this study are heterogeneous in many dimensions, such as size and sector, as well as gender and ethnicity of the founder. What role does heterogeneity between organisations play with regard to interorganisational trust and control? This was a study of a customer choice market. As studies on different kinds of public markets increase, a comparative approach would be relevant.

This paper has focused on the interaction of boundary spanners as embedded in different organisational systems. However, it gives rise to questions regarding the impact of the macro level in terms of changes in the political, legal and cultural situation. Further studies might preferably analyse policy documents and the media discourse in relation to individual and organisational trust–control processes.

Acknowledgements

The authors wish to thank the editors as well as the anonymous reviewers for their feedback and support in improving this paper. The authors also wish to thank professor emerita Elisabeth Sundin for introducing us to the context and the study of public sector transformation.

Disclosure statement

No potential conflict of interest was reported by the authors.

Funding

This work was supported by FORTE [Grant Number 2006-1524]; Sweden's Innovation Agency, VINNOVA: [Grant Number 2014-03143, 2016-00418]; and Linnaeus University.

ORCID

Lena Högberg ⓘ http://orcid.org/0000-0003-3030-0314
Birgitta Sköld ⓘ http://orcid.org/0000-0002-1953-1325
Malin Tillmar ⓘ http://orcid.org/0000-0002-0130-4407

References

Ahrne, G., Aspers, P., & Brunsson, N. (2015). The organization of markets. *Organization Studies, 36*(1), 7–27.

Appuhami, R., & Perera, S. (2016). Management controls for minimising risk in public-private partnerships in a developing country. *Journal of Accounting & Organizational Change, 12*(3), 408–431.

Argento, D., & Peda, P. (2015). Interactions fostering trust and contract combinations in local public services provision. *International Journal of Public Sector Management, 28*(4/5), 335–351.

Berlin, J. (2006). *Beställarstyrning av hälso-och sjukvård: Om människor, marginaler och miljoner.* Gothenburg: Gothenburg University.

Bijlsma-Frankema, K., & Costa, A. C. (2005). Understanding the trust-control nexus. *International Sociology, 20*(3), 259–282.

Blomqvist, P., & Rothstein, B. (2000). *Välfärdsstatens nya ansikte: Demokrati och marknadsstyrning inom den offentliga sektorn.* Stockholm: Agora.

Bradach, J. L., & Eccles, R. G. (1989). Price, authority, and trust: From ideal types to plural forms. *Annual Review of Sociology, 15*, 97–118.

Bringselius, L. (2017). *Tillitsbaserad styrning och ledning: Ett ramverk. Samtal om tillit i styrning: En rapportserie med bidrag till Tillitsdelegationen.* Stockholm: Regeringskansliet, Finansdepartementet.

Brown, T. L., Potoski, M., & Van Slyke, D. M. (2007). Trust and contract completeness in the public sector. *Local Government Studies, 33*(4), 607–623.

Bryson, J. M., Crosby, B. C., & Middleton Stone, M. (2006). The design and implementation of cross-sector collaborations: Propositions from the literature. *Public Administration Review, 66*(1), 44–55.

Bryson, J. M., Crosby, B. C., & Middleton Stone, M. (2015). Designing and implementing cross-sector collaborations: Needed and challenging. *Public Administration Review, 75*(5), 647–663.

Cäker, M., & Siverbo, S. (2011). Management control in public sector joint ventures. *Management Accounting Research, 22*(4), 330–348.

Chen, C.-H. (2009). Antecedents of contracting-back-in. *Administration & Society, 41*(1), 101–126.

Child, J. (1998). Trust and international strategic alliances: The case of Sino-foreign joint ventures. In C. Lane & R. Bachmann (Eds.), *Trust within and between organizations* (pp. 214–272). Oxford: Oxford University Press.

Choudhury, E. (2008). Trust in administration. *Administration & Society, 40*(6), 586–620.

Christensen, T., Laegreid, P., Roness, P. G., & Røvik, K. A. (2007). *Organization theory and the public sector: Instrument, culture and myth.* London: Routledge.

Clarkson, M. E. (1995). A stakeholder framework for analyzing and evaluating corporate social performance. *Academy of Management Review, 20*(1), 92–117.

Costa, A. C., & Biljsma-Frankema, K. (2007). Trust and Control Interrelations. *Group & Organization Management, 32*(4), 392–406.

Das, T. K., & Teng, B. (1998). Between trust and control: Developing confidence in partner cooperation in alliances. *Academy of Management, 23*(3), 491–512.

Das, T. K., & Teng, B. (2001). Trust, control, and risk in strategic alliances: An integrated framework. *Organization Studies, 22*(2), 251–283.

Deakin, S., & Wilkinson, F. (1998). Contract Law and the economics of interorganizational trust. In C. Lane & R. Bachmann (Eds.), *Trust within and between organizations: Conceptual issues and empirical applications* (pp. 146–172). Oxford: Oxford University Press.

Ditillo, A., Liguori, M., Sicilia, M., & Steccolini, I. (2015). Control patterns in contracting-out relationships: It matters what you do, not who you are. *Public Administration, 93*(1), 212–229.

Edelenbos, J., & Eshuis, J. (2012). The interplay between trust and control in governance processes. *Administration & Society, 44*(6), 647–674.

Edelenbos, J., & Klijn, E.-H. (2007). Trust in complex decision-making networks. *Administration & Society, 39*(1), 25–50.

Eisenhardt, K. M., & Graebner, M. E. (2007). Theory building from cases: Opportunities and challenges. *Academy of Management Journal, 50*(1), 25–32.

Erlandsson, S., Storm, P., Strads, A., Szebehely, M., & Trydegård, G.-B. (2013). Marketising trends in Swedish eldercare: Competition, choice and calls for stricter regulation. In G. Meagher & M. Szebehely (Eds.), *Marketisation in Nordic Eldercare* (pp. 23–84). Stockholm: Stockholm University.

European Commission. (2017). *Public procurement*. Retrieved from http://ec.europa.eu/trade/policy/accessing-markets/public-procurement

Ferlie, E., Ashburner, L., Fitzgerald, L., & Pettigrew, A. (1996). *The new public management in action*. Oxford: Oxford University Press.

Ferrin, D. L., Bligh, M. C., & Kohles, J. C. (2007). Can I trust you to trust me?. *Group & Organization Management, 32*(4), 465–499.

Fukuyama, F. (1996). *Trust: The social virtues and the creation of prosperity*. London: Penguin Books.

Gambetta, D. (1988). Can we trust trust? In D. Gambetta (Ed.), *Trust: Making and breaking cooperative relationships* (pp. 213–237). New York, NY: Blackwell.

Getha-Taylor, H. (2012). Cross-sector understanding and trust. *Public Performance & Management Review, 36*(2), 216–229.

Goodsell, C. T. (2006). Conflating forms of separation in administrative ethics. *Administration & Society, 38*(1), 135–141.

Hodge, G., & Greve, C. (2007). Public – private partnerships: An international performance review. *Public Administration Review, 67*(3), 545–558.

Högberg, L., & Mitchell, C. (2015). Mixed embeddedness, opportunity structures and opportunity tension – re-agenting the embedded entrepreneur *XXIX RENT conference*, Zagreb.

Huque, A. S. (2005). Contracting out and trust in the public sector: Cases of management from Hong Kong. *Public Organization Review, 5*, 69–84.

Inkpen, A. C., & Currall, S. C. (2004). The coevolution of trust, control, and learning in joint ventures. *Organization Science, 15*, 586–599.

Johns, G. (2006). The essential impact of context on organizational behavior. *Academy of Management Review, 31*(2), 386–408.

Kastberg, G. (2005). *Kundvalsmodeller. En studie av marknadsskapare och skapade marknader i kommuner och landsting*. Gothenburg: Gothenburg University.

Kastberg, G. (2016). Trust and control in network relations: A study of a public sector setting. *Financial Accountability & Management, 32*(1), 0267–4424.

Kim, S. (2005). The role of trust in the modern administrative state. *Administration & Society, 37*(5), 611–635.

Le Grand, J. (1991). Quasi-markets and social policy. *The Economic Journal, 101*(408), 1256–1267.

Lewis, J. D., & Weigert, A. (1985). Trust as a social reality. *Social Forces, 63*(4), 967–985.

Li, P. P. (2012). When trust matters the most: The imperatives for contextualising trust research. *Journal of Trust Research, 2*(2), 101–106.

Local Government Act. (1991:900). SFS. The Swedish Code of Statutes (official Swedish government publication containing all current laws).

LOU. (1992:1528). The Swedish Public Procurement Act. SFS. The Swedish Code of Statutes.

LOV. (2008:962). The Act on System of Choice in the Public Sector. SFS. The Swedish Code of Statutes.

Luhmann, N. (1979). *Trust and power*. New York, NY: Wiley.

Mannion, R., & Smith, P. (1998). How providers are chosen in the mixed economy of community care. In W. Bartlett, J. A. Roberts, & J. Le Grand (Eds.), *A revolution in social policy: Quasi market reforms in the 1990s* (pp. 111–131). Bristol: Policy Press.

Milbourne, L., & Cushman, M. (2013). From the third sector to the big society: How changing UK government policies have eroded third sector trust. *VOLUNTAS: International Journal of Voluntary and Nonprofit Organizations, 24*, 485–508.

Möllering, G. (2001). The nature of trust: From Georg Simmel to a theory of expectation, interpretation and suspension. *Sociology, 35*(2), 403–420.

Möllering, G. (2005). The trust/control duality. *International Sociology, 20*(3), 283–305.

Münscher, R., & Kühlmann, T. M. (2012). Using critical incident technique in trust research. In F. Lyon, G. Möllering, & M. N. K. Saunders (Eds.), *Handbook of research methods on trust* (pp. 210–222). Cheltenham: Edward Elgar.

Neu, D. (1991). Trust, contracting and the prospectus process. *Accounting, Organization & Society, 16* (3), 243–256.

Nooteboom, B. (1996). Trust, opportunism and governance: A process and control model. *Organization Studies, 17*(6), 985–1010.

Norén, L. (2003). *Valfrihet till varje pris: Om design av kundvalsmarknader inom skola och omsorg.* Göteborg: Bokförlaget BAS.

Oomsels, P., & Bouckaert, G. (2014). Studying interorganizational trust in public administration. *Public Performance & Management Review, 37*(4), 577–604.

Oomsels, P., & Bouckaert, G. (2017). Interorganizational trust in Flemish public administration: Comparing trusted and distrusted interactions between public regulates and public regulators. In F. Six & K. Verhoest (Eds.), *Trust in regulatory regimes* (pp. 80–114). Cheltenham: Edward Elgar.

Pollitt, C., & Bouckaert, G. (2011). *Public management reform: A comparative analysis-new public management, governance, and the Neo-Weberian state.* Oxford: Oxford University Press.

Prasad, A., & Prasad, P. (2002). The coming of age of interpretive organizational research. *Organizational Research Methods, 5*(1), 4–11.

Rousseau, D. M., Sitkin, S. B., Burt, R. S., & Camerer, C. (1998). Not so different after all: a cross-discipline view of trust. *Academy of Management Review, 23*(3), 393–404.

Rus, A., & Iglic, H. (2005). Trust, governance, and performance: The role of institutional and interpersonal trust in SME development. *International Sociology, 20*(3), 371–391.

Schilke, O., & Cook, K. S. (2013). A cross-level process theory of trust development in interorganizational relationships. *Strategic Organization, 11*(3), 281–303.

Singh, A., & Prakash, G. (2010). Public–private partnerships in health services delivery. *Public Management Review, 12*(6), 829–856.

Sitkin, S. B. (1995). On the positive effects of legalization on trust. *Research on Negotiation in Organizations, 5*, 185–217.

Sitkin, S., & Stickel, D. (1996). The road to hell: The dynamics of distrust in an era of quality. In R. M. Kramer & T. R. Tyler (Eds.), *Trust in organizations* (pp. 166–195). Thousand Oaks, CA: Sage.

Six, F. (2013). Trust in regulatory relations. *Public Management Review, 15*(2), 163–185.

Social Service Act. (1980:620/2010:453). SFS. The Swedish Code of Statutes.

Stewart, J., & Ablong, T. (2013). When Australian defence procurement goes wrong: Improving outcomes in a troubled contractual environment. *The Economic and Labour Relations Review, 24*(2), 238–254.

Sundin, E., & Tillmar, M. (2010). *Uppföljning av "Eget val" inom hemtjänsten i Linköpings kommun: Utförarperspektiv.* FoU-rapport, 63:2010. Linköping: Linköpings universitet.

Sztompka, P. (1999). *Trust: A sociological theory.* Cambridge: Cambridge University Press.

ter Bogt, H., & Tillema, S. (2016). Accounting for trust and control: Public sector partnerships in the arts. *Critical Perspectives on Accounting, 37*, 5–23.

Tillmar, M. (2005). Breaking out of distrust: Preconditions for trust and cooperation between small businesses in Tanzania. In K. Bijlsma-Frankema & R. J. A. Klein Woolthuis (Eds.), *Trust under pressure: Empirical investigations of trust and trust building in uncertain circumstances* (pp. 54–79). Cheltenham: Edward Elgar.

Tillmar, M. (2006). Swedish tribalism and Tanzanian entrepreneurship: Preconditions for trust formation. *Entrepreneurship and Regional Development, 18*(March), 91–107.

Tillmar, M. (2009). No longer so strange? (Dis)trust in municipality–small business relationships. *Economic and Industrial Democracy, 30*(3), 401–428.

Tillmar, M., & Lindkvist, L. (2007). Cooperation against all odds. *International Sociology, 22*(3), 343–366.

Vadelius, E. (2015). *Paradoxernas marknad: en studie om företagande i hemtjänsten.* Karlstad: Karlstad University.

Vallentin, S., & Thygesen, N. (2017). Trust and control in public sector reform: Complementarity and beyond. *Journal of Trust Research, 7*(2), 150–169.

Vanneste, B. S. (2016). From interpersonal to interorganisational trust: The role of indirect reciprocity. *Journal of Trust Research, 6*(1), 7–36.

Vlaar, P. W. L., Van den Bosch, F. A. J., & Volberda, H. W. (2007). On the evolution of trust, distrust, and formal coordination and control in interorganizational relationships. *Group & Organization Management, 32*(4), 407–428.

Walker, R., Smith, P., & Adam, J. (2009). Making partnerships work: Issues of risk, trust and control for managers and service providers. *Health Care Analysis, 17*, 47–67.

Weibel, A. (2007). Formal control and trustworthiness *Group & Organization Management, 32*(4), 500–517.

Welter, F. (2011). Contextualizing entrepreneurship-conceptual challenges and ways forward. *Entrepreneurship Theory & Practice, 35*(1), 165–184.

Williamson, O. E. (1975). *Markets and hierarchies: Analysis and antitrust implications: A study in the economics of internal organization*. New York: Free Press.

Yin, R. K. (2013). *Case study research: Design and methods*. Thousand Oaks, CA: Sage.

Yttermyr, O. (2013). *Varför blev det (bara) en?: En studie av en offentlig marknad i förändring*. Linköping: Linköping University Electronic Press.

Zucker, L. (1986). Production of trust: Institutional sources of economic structure, 1840–1920. *Research in Organizational Behavior, 8*(1), 53–111.

Appendices

Appendix 1. Research published 1990–2017 on the trust–control dynamics within public sector IORs

Author(s) and year	Publication	Method	Type of IOR	Industry/country	Findings relating to trust–control dynamics (selected)
Mannion and Smith (1998)	*A Revolution in Social Policy: Quasi Market Reforms in the 1990s, (Bartlett, Roberts & Le Grand)*	Qualitative	Purchaser/Private providers Procurement	Care for the elderly England	Mechanisms influencing the assessment of the quality of a provider include: formal inspection, feedback from users; informal networks; and provider marketing. Qualitative issues are replaced by the concept of trust. p. 131
Huque (2005)	*Public Organization Review: A Global Journal*	Qualitative	Housing authority/Contractors Contracting-out Public/private	Housing Hong Kong	'Along with streamlining the procedures, increasing emphasis on accountability, and improving the system of monitoring, the answer seems to lie in the inculcation of a spirit of trust and cooperation between the principal and agent.' p. 81
Brown et al. (2007)	*Local Government Studies*	Qualitative	Contracting for-profit and non-profit partners	Refuse collection, social service provision USA	'The degree to which contracts are more or less complete is a function of numerous factors such as the duration of the contract, level of experience each contracting party has with one another, the risk tolerance levels of the parties, service characteristics, market competitiveness, the incentives employed, and the potential for unforeseen contingencies.' [...] ' ... the degree of contract completeness is contingent on the level of trust between government and its vendors.' [... a one-size-fits-all approach to writing contracts is not optimal.' p. 62
Chen (2009)	*Administration & Society*	Theoretical paper	Contracting-out relations		'Relational contracting complements the insufficiency of rational control.' p. 116 'Proposition 8: Failing to detect the need for balance between relational contract and formal contract can result in low performance and contracting failure.' p. 117
Walker, Smith, and Adam (2009)	*Health Care Analysis*	Qualitative interviews	Primary Care Partnership Private partners	Primary health care Australia	Informants' perspectives on risk and uncertainty, trust and control tended to be consistent with their position in the partner organisation. p. 65
Singh and Prakash (2010)	*Public Management Review*	Qualitative interviews	PPP – network	Health care India	'Power is asymmetrically distributed in the network, and there is greater reliance on formal mechanisms of co-ordination. However, for networks to be an

(*Continued*)

Continued.

Author(s) and year	Publication	Method	Type of IOR	Industry/country	Findings relating to trust–control dynamics (selected)
					effective way of governing, it is important to reduce the power asymmetry between the partners, and rely more on informal mechanisms of co-ordination and trust, and develop horizontal co-ordination and social capital in these networks.' p. 851
Čåker and Siverbo (2011)	*Management Accounting Research*	Qualitative cases	Joint ventures among public organisations	Waste disposal activities Sweden	'… vertical control packages are affected by: goodwill trust and competence trust; parent differences in management style and size in combination with control competence; parent diversification (low relatedness between the JV's activity and the parents' other activities); and the horizontal control package (e.g. rules for parent interaction and distribution of work). Horizontal control packages are affected by: goodwill trust, system trust and calculative trust; parent differences in size; and efforts to achieve equality.' […] '… trust is potentially unaffected by the introduction of formal controls…. trust has an inverted 'crowding out' effect on control. A high ambition to maintain trust leads to underdeveloped formal controls.' p. 330
Edelenbos and Eshuis (2012)	*Administration & Society*	Qualitative interviews	Community based /citizens – public managers – farmers	Spatial planning Netherlands	'the relationship between trust and control is multiform and has also shown that when dissected, how different forms of control may enhance or decrease different forms of trust and vice versa. In particular, … different coevolutionary pathways of trust and control exist.' p. 668 '… the coevolution of trust and control depends on the specific (initial) situation in which the relationship between trust and control unfolds. Trust and control are related through complex and contingent causation, resulting in divergent paths of coevolution.' p.669
Milbourne and Cushman (2013)	*Voluntas*	Qualitative interviews	Public authorities and/third sector providers of public services Procurement	Education for disengaged young people and service for children and youths England	'Drawing on examples from empirical studies in two English inner-city areas we explore ways in which power and controls exerted through dominant organizational cultures and arrangements undermine independent approaches, innovation and organisational learning across sectors. State bodies have taken trust in their actions as given while shifting responsibilities for service delivery and risks of failure to others.' p. 485 ' … increasing market

Six (2013)	*Public Management Review*	Theoretical paper	Regulatory relations	cultures and regulation have damaged cross-sector trust promoting divisive interests and risk-averse behaviours, restricting the local autonomy, innovation and community action presumed in the Big Society agenda.' p. 485 'SDT is used to build a model for the relation between regulator trust and control as they affect regulatee compliance. The model follows the perspective that control may complement trust in achieving internalization of regulator values by the regulatee and thus result in voluntary compliance. Such self-determined, voluntary compliance has a positive impact on regulator trust, which in turn has a positive effect on both regulate internalization of regulator values and regulator controls that enhance selfdetermination. This creates a reinforcing cycle. Next, several factors were discussed that affect the different variables in the cycle. These may further reinforce or dampen the cycle.' p. 179
Stewart and Ablong (2013)	*The Economic and Labour Relations Review*	Qualitative longitudinal interviews	PPP Procurement	'In these circumstances, tightening and sharpening processes and controls might have had its advantages. However, given the realities of defence procurement, it is hard to see that the problems of the system, many of which lie in the multiple purposes it tries to serve, can be fully resolved in this way. The need for both more flexibility and more accountability is evident. To bring these values into better balance requires processes that encourage, rather than discourage, communication, collaboration, trust and a more realistic sharing of risk.' p. 250
Argento and Peda (2015)	*International Journal of Public Sector Management*	Qualitative longitudinal interviews	IOR between local governments and service provision companies with different owner structure Externalised public service provision of water Estonia	The relationship between trust and contract, which can either be substitutes or complements, or eventually erode each other, is contingent upon the capacity of interacting individuals (and related organizations) to keep interests aligned in water services provision.' Abstract p. 335 ' ... mode and frequency of interactions between key actors within the underling governance setting foster different combinations of trust and contracts.' p. 348

(Continued)

Continued.

Author(s) and year	Publication	Method	Type of IOR	Industry/country	Findings relating to trust–control dynamics (selected)
Ditillo et al. (2015)	*Public Administration*	Quantitative questionnaire	Chief Executive Officers Contracting-out to private providers	Waste collection Homecare for the elderly Italy	'In the presence of contracting-out, market-, hierarchy-, and trust-based controls display different intensities, can coexist, and are explained by different variables.' p. 212
Appuhami and Perera (2016)	*Journal of Accounting & Organizational Change*	Qualitative interviews	PPP Management control systems	Power sector Sri Lanka	'While bureaucratic control was the predominantly used control pattern throughout the three phases (namely, selecting, building and operating) of the PPP, trust-based controls also played an important role. Market controls on the other hand played, somewhat, a nominal role, particularly in the selecting phase of the project.' p. 425
Kastberg (2016)	*Financial Accountability & Management*	Qualitative longitudinal interviews	Network between public organisational units and a public shared service centre	IT Sweden	'...compared to actors in previous studies of dyadic relationships in the private sector, actors in network relations seem to consider trust a risky option. It is less tempting to rely on a certain party when that party in turn is entangled with other parties. This situation causes a more intensive use of formal control. Another result is that increased trust between two parties might lead to more emphasis on formal control by a third party.' p. 33 'Formal control was used both to signal trust and to limit the growth of trust; formal control sometimes also had side effects that problematized relations.' p. 52 'As the case indicates, divergent views of control initiatives might exist between parties and these variances might also affect others (third parties)' p. 53
ter Bogt and Tillema (2016)	*Critical Perspectives on Accounting*	Qualitative interviews	Partnership between theatres and municipalities Subsidies	Theatres Netherlands	'...trust is a very important element in the control of these public sector partnerships. The importance of trust is reinforced because the civil servants and aldermen are aware of the difficulty of expressing the objectives of the municipal cultural policies in quantitative terms. The same holds true for the contribution of the theatre's outputs and outcomes to realizing these objectives.' p. 19 'However, the low measurability of the theatres' outputs and outcomes complicates the municipalities' control as based on performance agreements and accounting information. This complication increases the role of trust.' p. 5

Appendix 2. Critical incidents manifesting the coevolution of (dis)trust and control in the Fieldtown case.

Time	Phase 1	Phase 2	Phase 3	Phase 4	Phase 5	Phase 6
Level of organisational systems						
Elderly care services committee	The customer choice model is launched with a vision of diversity in small providers.	Demonstrates trust in providers that are authorised and partial trust in Khabat who is partially authorised.	Sets a goal to increase the number of small providers.	Maintains objective of supporting small providers.	A new majority with a new agenda: quality over provider diversity. Decides on control programme.	Terminates the contracts of seven providers who fail to meet the requirements. Decides to keep the customer choice model.
Elderly care services department	Authorisation criteria are set at a level to enable small firms to be authorised.	Authorisation followed by punctual follow ups – errors are corrected continuously.	Supports small providers via an educational approach.	Rewrites authorisation criteria to hinder opportunistic behaviour.	A general control operation is conducted comprising all providers.	The contracts of seven providers (35%) are terminated. A new control system is implemented and authorisation criteria revised.
Small private providers (category)	Difficult to compete with large providers, few make it.	First of small providers with a niche strategy is authorised to provide personal care.	Several small providers apply for authorisation.	Competition amongst small providers increases as new firms apply.	All providers are reviewed; those who do not meet the criteria are revised again.	Seven contracts are terminated. Subject to increased continuous controls. New firms are authorised.
Level of boundary spanners						
Municipal officers: first Kristina and Ulla then Eva and Margareta	Expresses trust in established providers (competence). (E in 2014)	Suggests only partial authorisation of Khabat (lack of formal competence). Continuous dialogue to make him stick to the contract. (K and U)	Trust in small providers is undermined by perceived lack of competence. (E and M)	Small providers act in ways that were not intended and hence they suggest that authorisation criteria are revised. (E)	Increased distrust based on evidence of opportunistic behaviour by some providers (in addition to lack of competence in some providers). (E and M)	(M) Expresses distrust in providers whose contracts are terminated. Expresses trust in the remaining providers, both competence and goodwill, but also based on controls (deterrence trust).
Khabat	Applies for authorisation in late 2010.	Is partially authorised but unhappy with the decision; strives for more hours and to be fully trusted.	The firm grows substantially in terms of clients and staff. Seeks full authorisation again but is rejected.	Distrusts the municipality based on perceived discrimination and suspicion of corruption.	Full authorisation is once more denied Is subject to review and fails in both first and second rounds.	Is excluded from the customer choice system as a final statement of distrust. Distrusts the municipality in return. Takes the case to court but loses.
Aminah	Employed by the municipality.	Employed by the municipality.	Employed by the municipality.	Applies for authorisation and is fully authorised despite lack of formal qualifications.	Is subject to review and subsequently approved.	Grows as other firms fail the control efforts but distrusts the municipality for lack of trust in small providers with immigrant background.

Job insecurity, employee anxiety, and commitment: The moderating role of collective trust in management

Wen Wang, Kim Mather and Roger Seifert

ABSTRACT

This article examines the moderating effect of collective trust in management on the relation between job insecurity (both objective and subjective) and employee outcomes (work-related anxiety and organisational commitment). This is contextualised in the modern British workplace which has seen increased employment insecurity and widespread cynicism. We use matched employer-employee data extracted from the British Workplace Employment Relations Survey (WERS) 2011, which includes over 16,000 employees from more than 1100 organisations. The multilevel analyses confirm that objective job insecurity (loss of important elements of a job such as cuts in pay, overtime, training, and working hours) are significantly correlated with high levels of work-related anxiety and lower levels of organisational commitment. These correlations are partially mediated by subjective job insecurity (perception of possible job loss). More importantly, collective trust in management (a consensus of management being reliable, honest and fair) significantly attenuates the negative impact of objective job insecurity on organisational commitment, and reduces the impact of subjective job insecurity on work-related anxiety. Theoretical and practical implications and limitations of these effects are discussed.

Introduction

Workers increasingly feel job insecurity at most workplaces in the UK due to a combination of the 2008 economic crisis and subsequent long recession, shifts in technology that are creating new, while destroying old jobs, and the rapid deployment of casual employment contracts across the skill spectrum. Such insecurity is born out of both experiencing actual loss of parts of the job and from expectations of future job loss, and can result in greater levels of stress, reduced organisational commitment, and an overall reduction in worker performance. We seek to show that this tendency can be partly offset if, and only if, there is collective, as opposed to individual, employee trust in management.

Job insecurity has been theoretically and empirically tested as a stressor rather than as a motivator (for a review see De Witte, 2005; Sverke, Hellgren, & Näswall, 2006). However, the actual relationship between job insecurity and employee attitudes and behaviour has been empirically found to vary across studies, with significant negative, little or even positive relation (Furaker & Berglund, 2014; Hellgren, Sverke, & Isaksson, 1999; Loi, Ngo, Zhang, & Lau, 2011; Staufenbiel & König, 2010; Wong, Wong, Ngo, & Lui, 2005). Our argument is that genuine job insecurity leads to anxiety, distress, and ultimately impacts on workers' performance. The above controversial findings are partly due to the subjective job insecurity measurement used, which was found to be shaped by personal traits, types of contract, and work environments (De Witte, 2005; Lam, Liang, Ashford, & Lee, 2015). We endeavour to screen subjective 'noises' out through distinguishing objective job insecurity (real experiences of loss of job elements) from subjective job insecurity (perceptions of potential job loss).

Such differentiations allow us to disentangle the effect of job insecurity by nature (objective or subjective) and on that basis; we can explore organisational practices which may attenuate its negative impact on employee outcomes. Drawing on trust literature insights from both employment relations (Grey & Garsten, 2001) and the psychology of trust (Dirks & Ferrin, 2001), we examine the effect of Collective Trust in Management (CTM), a consensus of members of staff which reflects organisational management practices, on the relationship between job insecurity and employee outcomes. Methodologically, we follow an alternative approach that consists of aggregating individual perceptions of trust in management (Alfes, Shantz, & Truss, 2012; Innocenti, Pilati, & Peluso, 2011). Consistent ratings on management among employees reflect a value or principle of organising (McEvily, Perrone, & Zaheer, 2003) and represent workplace practices (Kuenzi & Schminke, 2009), which is a property of an organisation and can be used to differentiate organisations (Schreurs, Guenter, van Emmerik, Notelaers, & Schumacher, 2015). This study therefore expands the research into group level trust within the organisational context (Dirks & Ferrin, 2001; Fulmer & Gelfand, 2012; Siebert, Martin, Bozic, & Docherty, 2015).

This current study is located in the UK at a time when one in seven British workers has been laid-off since the 2008 economic crash (Peacock, 2013). These proposed relationships were tested with matched employee-employer data compiled from the British Workplace Employment Relations Survey (WERS) 2011. This is a national representative data set that has been designed to monitor employment relations in the UK since 1980 (Lai, Saridakis, Blackburn, & Johnstone, 2015). The rest of the paper is organised as follows: first we present a review of job insecurity and employee outcomes before discussing the potential moderator of collective trust in management. There is then a description of the research methods before we present our empirical findings. Finally we discuss our findings, noting their theoretical and practical implications.

Job insecurity, work related anxiety, and organisational commitment

Most job insecurity studies have focused on a subjective perception of job loss resulting from the threatening objective conditions in which people work, such as organisational downsizing and the prevalence of 'flexible' contracts (Ashford, Lee, & Bobko, 1989; De Witte, 2005; Ellonen & Nätti, 2013; Keim, Landis, Pierce, & Earnest, 2014; Wang & Heyes, 2017). Hidden job insecurity has been overlooked although recognised

(Greenhalgh & Rosenblatt, 1984) as the loss of 'valued job features' at the workplace. In spite of a lack of consensus on what are regarded as 'valued job features', researchers have generally agreed that deterioration in working conditions and pay are among core elements (Gallie, Felstead, Green, & Inanc, 2017; Sverke et al., 2006). For example Hellgren et al. (1999) developed the construct of qualitative job insecurity, that is to say, losing important aspects of one's job, in order to distinguish from subjective (quantitative) perception of job loss. The term job status insecurity has also been used to emphasise the perception of loss of core elements of a job (Gallie et al., 2017). Based on these extant literatures, the present study further develops objective job insecurity as the actual personal experience of losing important aspects of one's job: reduction in pay, working hours, overtime and training. Meanwhile, subjective job insecurity is also included to measure the *perceived* continuity (security) of the current job (Heaney, Israel, & House, 1994, p. 243).

According to mainstream HRM accounts there are positive links between engaged, highly-committed workers and high levels of organisational performance (Marchington, Wilkinson, Donnelly, & Kynighou, 2016; Truss, Mankin, & Kellinher, 2012). As a result, conventional wisdom is that subjective job insecurity is positively associated with work-based anxiety (Blom, Richter, Hallsten, & Svedberg, 2018; De Witte et al., 2010; Erlinghagen, 2008). It has been assumed that job insecurity delivers lower levels of organisational commitment and other negative attitudes towards work and the workplace (Ashford et al., 1989). However, contrary to these general beliefs, empirical studies have shown differing results. For example, Hellgren et al. (1999) found that both qualitative and quantitative subjective insecurity have no impact on job satisfaction and turnover intention when controlled for affectivity. A few studies even show a positive relationship between subjective job insecurity and organisational citizenship behaviour (Furaker & Berglund, 2014; Wong et al., 2005). Two possible reasons were proposed that may explain such apparently contradictory findings: firstly, job insecurity is predominately researched as a subjective perception in which personal traits (locus of control and negative affectivity) were found to play a significant part in the reported job insecurity instead of an adverse objective situation (decreased organisational profit report) (De Witte, 2005). Secondly, the popular definition used originated from Greenhalgh and Rosenblatt (1984, p. 440), 'the perceived powerlessness to maintain the desired continuity in a threatened job situation', and may not apply with equal conviction to survey participators (Lam et al., 2015). That is to say that a job insecurity event may not exist when surveyed, or that participants may voluntarily choose a temporary job which suits their present situation but which involves permanent feelings of powerlessness.

Nearly four million workers in the UK have been made redundant since the 2008 financial crash and subsequent long recession (Peacock, 2013). This makes the threat to job security a particularly compelling and timely focus of study. There is an additional threat for those still in work in the form of losing valued features of their jobs (Gallie et al., 2017). Since 2009 two-thirds of employees have experienced a pay freeze (Gammel, 2012), and there have also been widespread reductions in overtime pay, working hours, training, non-wage benefits, and other terms and conditions of employment (Wang & Seifert, 2017). This has been made worse by the fact that some employees have been forced into debt as a consequence of enduring a pay freeze since 2008 (PSE, 2016). Job survivors have to do more with fewer resources (Burke & Cooper, 2000), and once exposed to downsizing, more cuts in job features tend to follow, triggering constant stress that is argued to have caused increasing reports of mental health problems (Klug, 2017, p. 3). These 'sacrifices' have been empirically found to negatively correlate with employees' work attitudes, such as job satisfaction and organisational commitment leading to, *inter alia*, increased absenteeism and poor performance (Brown, Gray, McHardy, & Taylor, 2015). Redundancy and cost-cutting measures can be seen as intentional and deliberate (Cameron, Freeman, & Mishra, 1991). We therefore conjecture that:

Hypothesis 1a: Objective job insecurity is positively correlated with work-related anxiety

Hypothesis 1b: Objective job insecurity is negatively correlated with organisational commitment

Subjective job insecurity is a perceptual phenomenon that varies in intensity even when employees are confronted by identical job threats (Greenhalgh & Rosenblatt, 1984; Hartley, Jacobson, Klandermans, & van Vuuren, 1991), and, as has been noted, is determined by personal, job, and organisational realities (Ashford et al., 1989). There is convincing evidence that the locus of control and negative affectivity are correlated with perceived job insecurity (for a review, see Sverke et al., 2006). Objective job insecurity, on the other hand, is the experience of losing valued elements of a job, and will therefore be positively correlated with subjective evaluations of job loss. In addition, since subjective job insecurity is determined by personal, work and other unobservable factors, when subjective job insecurity is included, it will reduce the impact of objective job insecurity on work-related attitudes. This leads to our Hypothesis 2.

Hypothesis 2a: Subjective job insecurity will partially mediate the relationships between objective job insecurity and work-related anxiety

Hypothesis 2b: Subjective job insecurity will partially mediate the relationships between objective job insecurity and organisational commitment

Collective trust in management, job insecurity and employee outcomes

Gould-Williams and Davies (2005) state that trust is an essential element of any positive exchange relationship and a necessary prerequisite for interaction in the face of uncertainty and vulnerability. This particularly matters when employees face job insecurity due to the power imbalance between management and employees. However, extant studies have revealed that the direct effect of trust on attitudinal outcomes is marginal and inconsistent (Dirks & Ferrin, 2002). A few moderating effect studies have focused on personal trust in supervisors. Investigations into the micro-level interactions between individual employees and their line managers are potentially problematic. First, supervisors act within a multilevel organisational context, their actions are permitted by the organisational setting; without understanding the organisational level of trust, investigations into the micro-level interactions between individual employees and their line managers are therefore rootless and unrealistic (Siebert et al., 2015). Second, the assumption of equal power between workers and managers does not reflect the reality of the employment relationship (Siebert et al., 2015). Instead the employment relationship is predicated on the principles of command and subordination (Kahn-Freund, 1954; Wedderburn, 1986), as this infers at best, deference (and fear of job loss), rather than trust.

This is particularly the case as the UK labour market has seen increased insecure employment and is characterised by a lack of alternative 'decent' jobs. Rubery (2015) highlights widespread patterns of distrust and broken promises as a consequence of job insecurity. This is underpinned by a wider climate of sustained downward pressure on both wages and pensions for many workers (ONS, 2015). Since 2010, many thousands of workers from across the public and the private sectors have been made redundant (Peacock, 2013), and this tends to make workers more cynical (Pugh, Skarlicki, & Passell, 2003). More generally, employer-led cost-cutting measures tend to be perceived negatively by employees and as a consequence they are less likely to exhibit trust, goodwill, and cooperation at work (Hudson, 2005).

Following Rousseau, Sitkin, Burt, and Camerer (1998, p. 395), the view taken here is that trust is a psychological state comprising the intention to accept vulnerability based upon positive expectations of the intentions or behaviour of another. In the organisational context, this so-called 'psychological contract' affects how employees assess the future behaviour of management, how employees interpret past management actions, and the motives underlying such actions (Dirks & Ferrin, 2001). In the employment relations context, trust is more accurately understood as being concerned with predictability in relation to the expected behaviour of management (Grey & Garsten, 2001), and to agree with the necessity to 'sacrifice' in hard times. This understanding and psychological state can be further strengthened by peer influence. The consensus of employees' evaluation of management's day-to-day labour management reflects the extent to which employees share a general judgment of management being predictable, reliable, and honest in their dealings and decision-making (McEvily et al., 2003). As Fox made clear, there is a close relationship between the ways in which work is organised as it shapes the workplace social relations that are subsequently characterised by 'patterns of trust and distrust generated by men's [sic] exercise of power over others in the pursuit of their own purposes' (1974, p. 15). This trust gained over a long period of direct and indirect interactions between employees and the management team can reinforce the 'positive moral connotations' of 'good' management (Grey & Garsten, 2001). Therefore, collective trust in management reflects a general perception of management being predictable and fair. When sufficient members of staff share the same view in management, it mirrors organisational practices, and is the property that differentiates organisations (Schreurs et al., 2015). Such a 'collective' measure reduces the importance of individual worker characteristics (age, gender, skill level, union affiliation, and seniority) on the formation of trust relations, and allows the emphasis to be on worker-centered reactions to actual management behaviour. In other words the decisions of senior managers as the collective expression of employer policy, *ceteris paribus*, impact equally upon all staff in terms of job (in)security and therefore all staff will tend to share the similar attitudes towards relevant trust in management intentions.

When there are high levels of collective trust in management, employees have a shared belief that the management team's future behaviour is both predictable and positive (Dirks & Ferrin, 2001). This provides employees with a sense of control over the future of the workplace, and, therefore, it may reduce the impact of subjective job insecurity on work-related anxiety. For example, Mishra and Spreitzer (1998) explain that trust in management can reduce the extent of the assessment to which organisational downsizing is seen by employees to be a threat. Furthermore, when employees perceive that down-sizing has been handled unfairly their responses are likely to be negative, which intensifies anxiety (Brockner et al., 2004). Meanwhile, in workplaces with high levels of trust, when employees believe sacrificing cherished elements of one's job, objective job insecurity, is necessary for the survival of the organisation and the related need to hoard skilled staff (Goodridge, Haskel, & Wallis, 2013), they may even support employers' decisions, thereby minimising any negative impact on organisational commitment caused by such sacrifices. If employees collectively share a lower trust in management, they may become suspicious and cynical about adverse changes. In the case of objective job insecurity, it may be construed as management taking advantage of employees in a difficult economic climate; and any promises made by management to reinstate these benefits becomes uncertain. This may then worsen the impact of subjective and objective job insecurity on employees' outcomes.

We therefore propose that:

Hypothesis H3a: Collective trust in management (CTM) can moderate the positive correlation between objective job insecurity and work-related anxiety, such that the positive correlation is weaker when CTM is higher.

Hypothesis H3b: Collective trust in management (CTM) can moderate the positive correlation between subjective job insecurity and work-related anxiety, such that the positive correlation is weaker when CTM is higher.

Hypothesis H4a: Collective trust in management (CTM) can moderate the negative correlation between objective job insecurity and organisational commitment, such that the negative correlation is weaker when CTM is higher.

Hypothesis H4b: Collective trust in management (CTM) can moderate the negative correlation between subjective job insecurity and organisational commitment, such that the negative correlation is weaker when CTM is higher.

Method

Data and sample

The matched employer-employee data, extracted from the 2011 Workplace Employment Relations Study (WERS, 2014) in the UK, is used as the basis for this study. WERS 2011 is the sixth in a series of national surveys on employment relations at the British workplace. It collects data from employers and employee representatives through face-to-face structured interviews and up to 25 employees per organisation through a self-completion survey on paper or online in a representative sample of workplaces.

The WERS 2011 dataset comprises 21,981 employee respondents with a maximum 25 each from the associated 2680 organisations. We only include organisations with more than 10 valid responses of permanent contracted employees. This former criterion was considered to be more appropriate to measure group members' shared perceptions at the organisational level (Drexler, 1977; Whitener, 2001), and the latter ensures that only employees who have contractual job security were included. This final sample was thus reduced to 16,574 valid respondents, representing 1149 organisations. The average number of respondents per organisation is 16 (range = 10–25).

Measures

Job insecurity: includes measurement of both Subjective and Objective Job Insecurity (SJI and OJI). The former gauges the personal perception of the likelihood of losing one's job measured by the rating with regard to the extent that these permanently contracted employees feel their employment is secure (reversely coded as 1 = strongly agree; 5 = strongly disagree) (Heany, et al.,1994). The latter is measured by personal experience of cuts in a number of 'valued job features' (Gallie et al., 2017; Hellgren et al., 1999; Sverke et al., 2006) including restricted access to training, paid overtime, wages being frozen or cut, and reduced working hours during the recent recession (0 = not at all; 4 = a great deal). OJI and SJI have a ICC(1) of 0.17 and 0.23 respectively, indicating members of the same organisation face similar job threatening practices and share this similar perception to a considerable extent.

Work related anxiety: was assessed by using items (Warr, 1990) that reflect the frequency of six job-related emotional states: tense, depressed, worried, gloomy, uneasy and miserable in the WERS data (Wood, Van Veldhoven, Croon, & de Menezes, 2012). This measure has a Cronbach's alpha of 0.85. Anxiety is the mean of these six items reported by individual team members.

Organisational commitment

In line with other empirical work based on WERS data (Brown et al., 2015; Brown, McHardy, McNabb, & Taylor, 2011; Saridakis, Muñoz Torres, & Johnstone, 2013), this construct was assessed using three items which show the extent to which employees share the same values of the organisation, feel loyal to, and proud of working for the organisation. The measure had a Cronbach's alpha of 0.77. Organisational commitment is measured by the mean score on these three items.

Collective Trust in Management (CTM)

Following other empirical studies based on WERS data (Bryson, 2001; Timming, 2012), individual trust in management was assessed by using three items asking respondents to rate the degree to which management can be relied upon to keep their promises, deal with employees honestly, and treat employees fairly (1 = strongly disagree to 5 = strongly agree). This measure has a Cronbach's alpha of 0.90. The mean of these three items was used to measure individual perceptions of trust in management. Collective trust in management (CTM) was treated as a conceptual organisational variable and assumed to significantly differ across organisations. It involves the aggregated degree of trust shared with sufficient consensus among members in an organisation (Fulmer & Gelfand, 2012; Jiang & Probst, 2015). Aggregation statistics were computed to validate this measure. The Average Deviation (AD) index obtained was less than 0.38, which was below the threshold of 0.87 (Burke & Dunlap, 2002). The $r_{wg(J)}$ >0.72 was above the conventional accepted value 0.7 (James, Demaree, & Wolf, 1993), together with the values of ICC(1) and ICC(2) being 0.16 and 0.72, respectively. These indices provided sufficient justification that this aggregation can be used to reflect organisational practices in general and to differentiate organisations (Schreurs et al., 2015).

Control variables

Individual factors were included since they were empirically reported to affect perceptions of job insecurity, employee anxiety and attitudes toward one's organisation, such as gender, age, job tenure, and managerial role (Ashford et al., 1989; Sverke, Hellgren, & Näswall, 2002). Over 40% of respondents in the sample are male workers, the average age is 44, and almost one third of the sample has a managerially related role. The average job tenure in the sample is 8 years. The average age of organisations in the sample is 45, and 40% of employees are from the public sector.

Methods of analysis

To test the interaction effect hypothesised, a moderated mediation modelling was applied following simplified steps outlined by Langfred (2004). Since employees are nested within each organisation with the assumption that organisational practices and workplace environment characteristics influence an individual's subjective perceptions, we therefore applied a hierarchical multilevel modelling approach which takes into account the dependent nature of the measurements at both individual and organisational levels (Hox, Moerbeek, & van de Schoot, 2017; Jiang & Probst, 2015). We used STATA 13 to estimate models (one for each outcome variable). The between-organisation variance explained by the variables and the deviance statistics (-2 Log likelihood) were reported (Snijders & Bosker, 2012).

Results

Preliminary analyses

Table 1 provides means, standard deviation, ICC values when appropriate, and correlations. ICC(1) for organisational commitment and anxiety is 0.16 and 0.07 respectively, denoting considerable variance in employees' organisational commitment determined at the organisational level; while individual characteristics largely attribute to reported anxiety. To check for multi-collinearity, Variance Inflation Factor (VIF) scores are less than 2 (not exceeding the threshold value of 4), suggesting that multi-collinearity is not a concern for the regression.

Empirical results

There are two moderated mediation models in this study to examine determinates of work-related anxiety in Table 2 and organisational commitment in Table 3. These models are tested through a series of hierarchical multilevel linear regressions based on the simplified steps recommended by Langfred (2004) and Jiang and Probst (2015). Since the mediator regression is the same for both models, it is only included in Table 2.

The objective of 'Mediation step 1' is to establish the relationship between OJI and employee outcomes in the absence of SJI (the mediator), in the same manner that CTM and OJI should interact when SJI is not included. Step 1 of 'Mediation step 1' in both tables shows that OJI is significantly and positively correlated with individual reported anxiety ($b = 0.19$, $p < 0.001$), but negatively and significantly correlated with organisational commitment ($b = -0.14$, $p < 0.001$). This provides empirical evidence to support hypotheses 1a and 1b.

Table 1. Statistics and correlations on main variables in WERS2011.

Variables	Mean(S.D.)	ICC(1)	ICC(2)	1	2	3	4	5	6	7	8	9
1 Gender	0.44(0.49)			1								
2 Age	44(12)			0.03**	1							
3 Having supervisory duty	0.33(0.46)			0.05**	0.04**	1						
4 Job tenure	7.98(5.46)			0.03**	0.40**	0.11**	1					
5 Objective job insecurity	0.67(0.85)	0.17	0.84	0.05**	0.04**	0.07**	0.14**	1				
6 Subjective job insecurity	2.53(1.10)	0.23	0.81	0.04**	0.05**	-0.05**	0.06**	0.25**	1			
7 Trust in management	2.96(0.53)	0.17	0.72	-0.21**	-0.03**	0.03**	-0.07**	-0.14**	-0.20**	1		
8 Org. commitment	3.74(0.88)	0.16	0.72	-0.08**	0.00	0.17**	-0.02**	-0.14**	-0.32**	0.22**	1	
9 Work related anxiety	2.04(0.82)	0.07	0.51	-0.04**	-0.04**	0.05**	0.05**	0.20**	0.32**	-0.17**	-0.33**	1

$** p < 0.01$, $* p < 0.05$.

Table 2. Hierarchical linear regression on anxiety.

Fixed effect (level 1)	Mediation Step 1: Anxiety			Mediation Step 2: Subjective job insecurity	Mediation Step 3: Anxiety		
	Step 1	Step 2	Step 3	Step 1	Step 1	Step 2	Step 3
Intercept (β_{01})	2.04***(0.03)	2.88***(0.07)	2.85***(0.07)	2.14***(0.03)	2.15***(0.03)	1.78***(0.11)	1.78***(0.11)
Age(γ_{10})	−0.00***(0.00)	−0.00***(0.00)	−0.00***(0.00)	0.00**(0.00)	−0.01***(0.00)	−0.01***(0.00)	−0.01***(0.00)
Male worker (γ_{20})	0.04***(0.01)	0.02(0.01)	0.02(0.01)	0.07***(0.01)	0.00(0.01)	0.00(0.01)	0.00(0.01)
Tenure	0.01***(0.00)	0.01***(0.00)	0.01***(0.00)	0.00(0.00)	0.01***(0.00)	0.01***(0.00)	0.01***(0.00)
Management position (γ_{30})	0.19***(0.01)	0.07***(0.01)	0.07***(0.01)	−0.17***(0.01)	0.11***(0.01)	0.11***(0.01)	0.11***(0.01)
Firm size		−0.01(0.01)	−0.01(0.01)	0.03***(0.01)	−0.01(0.01)	−0.01(0.01)	−0.01(0.01)
Firm age		−0.03***(0.01)	−0.02***(0.01)	−0.04***(0.01)	−0.02**(0.01)	−0.02**(0.00)	−0.02**(0.00)
Private sector		0.06***(0.02)	0.06***(0.02)	0.27***(0.03)	0.00(0.02)	0.01(0.02)	0.01(0.02)
Collective Trust in Management (CTM)		−0.24***(0.01)	−0.23***(0.01)		−0.17***(0.01)	−0.04(0.03)	−0.04(0.03)
Objective job insecurity		0.18***(0.01)	0.22***(0.01)	0.23***(0.01)	0.12***(0.01)	0.14***(0.05)	0.14***(0.05)
Subjective job insecurity					0.22***(0.01)	0.37***(0.03)	0.36***(0.03)
CTM*subjective job insecurity						−0.05***(0.01)	−0.05***(0.01)
CTM*objective job insecurity			−0.01(0.02)				−0.01(0.01)
Level 2 (intercept) (μ_1)	0.04	0.03	0.03	0.20	0.03	0.02	0.02
Level 1 (residual) (γ)	0.66	0.66	0.66	0.89	0.60	0.60	0.60
−2*Log likelihood	19084.27*2	18751.32*2	18750.32*2	21242.44*2	17497.97*2	17489.11*2	17488.11*2
Explained variance		25%	–		25%	33%	–
Number of organisations	1149	1089	1089	1089	1089	1089	1089
Number of employees	16,090	15,307	15,307	15,006	14,755	14,755	14,755

*$p < 0.1$, **$p < 0.05$, *** $p < 0.01$.

Table 3. Hierarchical linear regression on organisational commitment.

Fixed effect (level 1)	Mediation Step 1: Organisational commitment			Mediation Step 3&4: Organisational commitment		
	Step 1	Step 2	Step 3	Step 1	Step 2	Step3
Intercept (β_{01})	3.74***(0.05)	3.78***(0.05)	2.77***(0.09)	3.43***(0.09)	3.43***(0.09)	3.43***(0.09)
Age(γ_{10})	0.00***(0.00)	0.00***(0.00)	0.00***(0.00)	0.00***(0.00)	0.00***(0.00)	0.00***(0.00)
Male worker (γ_{20})	-0.11***(0.01)	-0.09***(0.01)	-0.09***(0.01)	-0.07***(0.01)	-0.07***(0.01)	-0.07***(0.01)
Tenure	-0.00***(0.00)	-0.00***(0.00)	-0.00***(0.00)	-0.00***(0.00)	-0.00***(0.00)	-0.00***(0.00)
Management position (γ_{30})	0.31***(0.01)	0.31***(0.01)	0.32***(0.01)	0.27***(0.01)	0.27***(0.01)	0.27***(0.01)
Firm size		-0.00(0.01)	-0.00(0.01)	-0.00(0.01)	-0.00(0.01)	-0.00(0.01)
Firm age		0.03***(0.01)	0.04***(0.01)	0.03***(0.01)	0.03***(0.01)	0.03***(0.01)
Private sector		-0.05***(0.02)	-0.06***(0.02)	-0.00(0.02)	-0.00(0.02)	-0.00(0.02)
Collective Trust in Management (CTM)		0.31***(0.02)	0.29***(0.02)	0.24***(0.02)	0.20***(0.02)	0.19***(0.02)
Objective job insecurity	-0.14***(0.00)	-0.13***(0.00)	-0.21***(0.00)	-0.07***(0.01)	-0.07***(0.01)	-0.18***(0.01)
Subjective job insecurity				-0.21***(0.01)	-0.25***(0.01)	-0.24***(0.01)
CTM*subjective job insecurity					0.01(0.01)	0.01(0.01)
CTM*objective job insecurity			0.04**(0.01)			0.04**(0.01)
Level 2 (intercept) (μ_1)	0.09	0.05	0.05	0.05	0.05	0.05
Level 1 (residual) (γ)	0.63	0.62	0.62	0.62	0.56	0.56
–2*Log likelihood	19132.67*2	18882.15*2	18880.32*2	17434.44*2	17433.07*2	17431.44*2
Explained variance	–	44%	–	44%	–	–
Number of organisations	1089	1089	1089	1089	1089	1089
Number of employees	15,591	15,591	15,307	15,006	15,006	15006

*p < 0.1, **p < 0.05, ***p < 0.01.

'Mediation Step 2' in Table 2 shows that OJI is positively and significantly correlated with SJI ($b = 0.23$, $p < 0.01$). The association between OJI and anxiety was reduced from ($b = 0.18$, $p < 0.01$) in Step 2 of 'Mediation Step 1: Anxiety' to ($b = 0.12$, $p < 0.01$) in Step 1 of 'Mediation Step 3&4: Anxiety' when SJI is included. In the same manner in Table 3, the association between OJI and organisational commitment was reduced from ($b = -0.13$, $p < 0.01$) in Step 2 of 'Mediation Step 1: Organisational commitment' to ($b = -0.07$, $p < 0.01$) in step 1 of 'Mediation Step 3&4: Organisation commitment' when SJI is included. Furthermore, the Sobel test shows that the mediation effect of SJI was statistically significant with approximately 40% of the total effect of OJI on anxiety and 53% of the total effect of OJI on organisational commitment. Overall, this provides support for Hypotheses 2a and 2b.

Hypothesis 3a predicts a negative moderating effect on the relationship between objective job insecurity and anxiety. This is tested in Step 3 of 'Mediation Step 1: Anxiety' in Table 2 where the interactive item of OJI and CTM shows an insignificant effect. Hypothesis 3b is tested by interacting SJI and CTM in step 2 of 'Mediation step 3&4: Anxiety', where the result shows a significant moderating effect ($b = -0.05$, $p < 0.01$) when controlling for CTM. Step 3 of 'Mediation step 3&4: Anxiety' is to establish whether the effect of the interaction of OJI and CTM is reduced when controlling for the interaction item of SJI and CTM, or vice versa (Langfred, 2004). The results show the moderating effect of CTM on the relationship between SJI and anxiety remains the same when including the interaction between OJI and CTM. This supports the moderating effect of hypothesis 3b.

In the same manner, we tested Hypothesis 4a and 4b in Table 3, and it shows there is a significant moderation effect of CTM, ($b = 0.04$, $p < 0.05$), on the relationship between OJI and organisational commitment in Step 3 of 'Mediation Step 1: organisational commitment'; but there is no such effect on the relationship between SJI and organisational commitment in Step 2 of 'Mediation Step 3&4: organisational commitment'. The former is not changed when the interactive item between SJI and CTM is included in Step 3 of "Mediation Step 3&4: organisational commitment'. This provides evidence to support the hypothesis 4a.

To examine the interaction of hypothesis 3a and 3b fully, a simple slope test was carried out and graphically presented in Figures 1 and 2. Figure 1 shows that employees' evaluation of work-related anxiety increases, *ceteris paribus*, with the increased perception of SJI. However, it is smaller in organisations with high levels of CTM. The difference in anxiety between organisations with high levels of trust and those with low levels of trust is statistically significant ($t = 4.24$, $p < 0.001$). Figure 2 shows that reported organisational commitment declined with increased OJI. The extent of deterioration, however, is much smaller in organisations characterised as having high levels of CTM than in those organisations with lower levels of CTM and the difference is statistically significant ($t = 3.35$, $p < 0.001$).

Discussion and conclusions

With really existing objective job insecurity rooted in the weak labour market, our analysis of the data confirms the detrimental impact of genuine job insecurity at the workplace as a stressor not a motivator (Lam et al., 2015; Sverke et al., 2006). Objective job insecurity leads

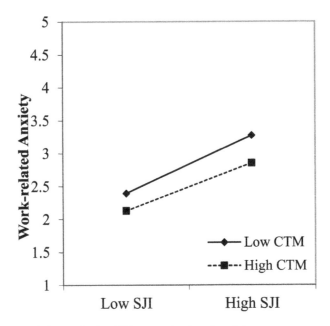

Figure 1. Subjective job insecurity by CTM on work-related anxiety.

to higher levels of subjective job insecurity; any cost-cutting measures do have an impact on perceived job insecurity, and therefore may result in lower cooperation (Hudson, 2005). Based on the above findings, we further reveal the value of collective trust in management (CTM) during hard times. Specifically, organisational commitment is less affected by objective job insecurity, such as pay cuts, reduction in working hours, training and benefits, in

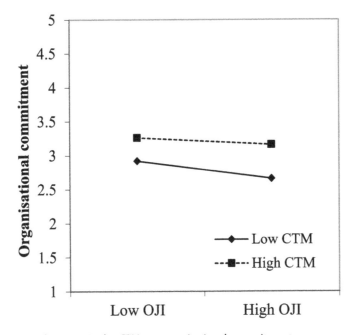

Figure 2. Objective job insecurity by CTM on organisational commitment.

organisations with high levels of CTM than those with low levels of CTM; and work-related anxiety caused by subjective job insecurity was smaller in organisations with high levels of CTM than those with low levels of CTM.

These different moderating mechanisms of CTM on the relationship between job insecurity and employee outcomes reflect the different impacts on employees of the nature of job insecurity. Objective Job Insecurity (OJI) is a genuine threat (entails financial costs) while Subjective Job Insecurity (SJI) is personal perception of job loss. When employees experience OJI, it tends to lead to high levels of anxiety due to financial pressures they shoulder on behalf of the organisation. For example, employees have been pushed into debt because of pay cuts in the public sector in the UK (PSE, 2016), and this fact cannot be masked even in organisations with a high level of CTM. However, in organisations with a high level of CTM, employees tend to believe that OJI measures undertaken by the management are necessary and these employees may even be prepared to sacrifice certain elements of their job, such as pay, pay related elements (reduction in working hours or overtime) and other benefits, in order to help the organisation (Wang & Seifert, 2017). Their intention is to stay and to work with the organisation during hard times. Therefore, CTM has a stronger moderating effect on the relationship between OJI and organisational commitment than on anxiety.

On the other hand, SJI is largely influenced by personality traits and other individual characteristics (De Witte, 2005). Our study lends empirical support to this position, as noted in Step 2 in Table 2. When individuals perceive job loss, this will lead to job search activities. Their intention is to leave, thus organisational commitment will be low even under high levels of CTM. However, CTM can reassure employees that management are predictable and are acting fairly when things go wrong, as for example in the case of a redundancy. In such circumstances high levels of CTM may help to attenuate the anxiety caused by perception of job loss. Therefore, CTM has a stronger moderating effect on the relationship between SJI and anxiety than on organisational commitment.

Our findings therefore add to the body of knowledge concerned with exploring productive roles of organisational capital (Tomer, 1987): a higher level of trust within organisations. We have endeavoured to capture this type of organisational capital through a consensus among employees of management being viewed as reliable and predictable. This is derived from the value and principle of organising by trust (McEvily et al., 2003). The value of high levels of trust is examined through the different moderating effects of collective trust in management on the relationship between job insecurity (by nature) and employee outcomes.

There are several limitations to note that also provide the basis for future research. First, it is possible that trust and perceptions of job security in large organisations may be heavily influenced by formalised, institutional arrangements, for example, formal dismissal and redundancy procedures, and the power of employees' representative bodies. Future studies could usefully seek to differentiate trust *in management* from trust *in organisations or systems* to investigate its antecedents and potential impact on employee outcomes. Third, our data is more likely to represent SMEs in terms of collective trust, with an upper limit of 25 respondents from each organisation. In order to more accurately measure a collective perception in large organisations, more respondents from the same organisation would be needed. It also has to be noted that for the purposes of our study subjective job insecurity is only measured by one item as a consequence of the way WERS data is collected. This leaves future studies to develop more sophisticated measurements that may further test the relationship proposed here.

We would suggest that our analysis raises important practical implications. It shows that when managers behave consistently, honestly, and fairly in their treatment of the workforce, then, and only then, will collective trust become part of the fabric of the organisation's employee relations systems (Schilke & Cook, 2013). This seems to be an important cue in workplaces which experience hardship. With high levels of collective trust in management, management was perceived as reliable, honest and fair. As a result, adverse changes threatening job security such as pay cuts, reduced benefits, and working hours have less impact on employees both in terms of work-related anxiety and commitment. This denotes a less pronounced effect on employees both mentally and attitudinally, and thus has a lower adverse effect on productivity. These findings are of particular relevance for SMEs whereby employers showed commitment to employment security (Lai et al., 2015). We suggest therefore that the results confirm the medium-term value of managers investing in their own strategic behaviour towards labour management issues such as worker-perceived consistency, fairness, and reliability. Whatever may occur at the national level of the economy, this study shows that micro-level firm behaviour can moderate the impact of negative practices on staff performance.

Acknowledgment

The authors acknowledge the 2011 Workplace Employment Relations Survey (WERS) sponsored by the Department for Business Innovation and Skills, the Economic and Social Research Council, the Advisory, Conciliation and Arbitration Service, the UK Commission for Employment and Skills and the National Institute of Economic and Social. The survey fieldwork was undertaken by The National Centre for Social Research, and the data was distributed by the Data Archive at the University of Essex. None of these organisations bears any responsibility for the authors' analysis and interpretations of the data. The authors also wish to acknowledge the diligent inputs from the Guest Editors, Dr Ashely Fulmer and Professor Kurt Dirks, and valuable suggestions from two anonymous reviewers.

Disclosure statement

No potential conflict of interest was reported by the authors.

References

Alfes, K., Shantz, A., & Truss, C. (2012). The link between perceived HRM practices, performance and well-being: The moderating effect of trust in the employer. *Human Resource Management Journal*, *22*(4), 409–427.

Ashford, S. J., Lee, C., & Bobko, P. (1989). Content, causes, and consequences of job insecurity: A theory-based measure and substantive test. *Academy of Management Journal*, *32*, 803–829.

Blom, V., Richter, A., Hallsten, L., & Svedberg, P. (2018). The associations between job insecurity, depressive symptoms and burnout: The role of performance-based self-esteem. *Economic and Industrial Democracy*, *39*(1), 48–63.

Brockner, J., Spreitzer, G., Mishra, A., Hochwarter, W., Pepper, L., & Weinberg, J. (2004). Perceived control as an antidote to the negative effects on survivors' organizational commitment and job performance. *Administrative Science Quarterly*, *49*, 76–100.

Brown, S., Gray, D., McHardy, J., & Taylor, K. (2015). Employee trust and workplace performance. *Journal of Economic Behavior & Organization*, *116*, 361–378.

Brown, S., McHardy, J., McNabb, R., & Taylor, K. (2011). Workplace performance, worker commitment, and loyalty. *Journal of Economics & Management Strategy*, *20*(3), 925–955.

Bryson, A. (2001). The foundation of 'partnership'? Union effects on employee trust in management. *National Institute Economic Review*, *176*(1), 91–104.

Burke, M. J., & Dunlap, W. P. (2002). Estimating interrater agreement with the average deviation index: A user's guide. *Organizational Research Methods*, *5*(2), 159–172.

Burke, R. J., & Cooper, C. L. (Eds.). (2000). *The organization in crisis: Downsizing, restructuring, and privatization*. Oxford: Blackwell Publishing.

Cameron, K., Freeman, S., & Mishra, A. (1991). Best practices in white-collar downsizing: Managing contradictions. *Academy of Management Executive*, *5*(3), 57–73.

De Witte, H. (2005). Job insecurity: Review of the international literature on definitions, prevalence, antecedents and consequences. *SA Journal of Industrial Psychology*, *31*(4), 1–6.

De Witte, H., De Cuyper, N., Handaja, Y., Sverke, M., Näswall, K., & Hellgren, J. (2010). Associations between quantitative and qualitative job insecurity and well-being: A test in Belgian banks. *International Studies of Management & Organization*, *40*(1), 40–56.

Dirks, K. T., & Ferrin, D. L. (2001). The role of trust in organizational settings. *Organization Science*, *12* (4), 450–467.

Dirks, K. T., & Ferrin, D. L. (2002). Trust in leadership: Meta-analytic findings and implications for research and practice. *Journal of Apllied Psychology*, *87*(4), 611–628.

Drexler, J. A. (1977). Organizational climate: Its homogeneity within organizations. *Journal of Applied Psychology*, *62*, 38–42.

Ellonen, N., & Nätti, J. (2013). Job insecurity and the unemployment rate: Micro-and macro-level predictors of perceived job insecurity among Finnish employees 1984–2008. *Economic and Industrial Democracy*, *36*(1), 51–71.

Erlinghagen, M. (2008). Self-perceived Job insecurity and social context: A multi-level analysis of 17 European countries. *European Sociological Review*, *24*(2), 183–197.

Fox, A. (1974). *Beyond contract: Work, trust and power relations*. London: Faber and Faber.

Fulmer, C. A., & Gelfand, M. J. (2012). At what level (and in whom) we trust: Trust across multiple organizational levels. *Journal of Management*, *38*(4), 1167–1230.

Furaker, B., & Berglund, T. (2014). Job insecurity and organizational commitment. *RIO: Revista Internacional de Organizaciones*, *13*, 163–186.

Gallie, D., Felstead, A., Green, F., & Inanc, H. (2017). The hidden face of job insecurity. *Work, Employment & Society*, *31*(1), 36–53.

Gammel, K. (2012, January 12). Two thirds of Britons subject to pay freeze. *The Telegraph*. Retrieved from http://www.telegraph.co.uk/finance/personalfinance/household-bills/9009438/Two-thirds-of-Britons-subject-to-pay-freeze.html

Goodridge, B., Haskel, P., & Wallis, G. (2013). Can intangible investment explain the UK productivity puzzle? *National Institute Economic Review*, *224*, R48–R58.

Gould-Williams, J., & Davies, F. (2005). Using social exchange theory to predict the effects of HRM practice on employee outcomes: An analysis of public sector works. *Public Management Review, 7*(1), 1–24.

Greenhalgh, L., & Rosenblatt, Z. (1984). Job insecurity: Toward conceptual clarity. *Academy of Management Review, 9,* 438–448.

Grey, C., & Garsten, C. (2001). Trust, control and post-bureaucracy. *Organization Studies, 22*(2), 229–250.

Hartley, J., Jacobson, D., Klandermans, B., & van Vuuren, T. (1991). *Job insecurity: Coping with jobs at risk.* London: Sage Publications.

Heaney, C., Israel, B., & House, J. (1994). Chronic job insecurity among automobile workers: Effects on job satisfaction and health. *Social Science and Medicine, 38*(10), 1431–1437.

Hellgren, J., Sverke, M., & Isaksson, K. (1999). A two-dimensional approach to job insecurity: Consequences for employee attitudes and well-being. *European Journal of Work and Organizational Psychology, 8*(2), 179–195.

Hox, J. J., Moerbeek, M., & van de Schoot, R. (2017). *Multilevel analysis: Techniques and applications.* New York and Hove: Routledge.

Hudson, M. (2005). Flexibility and the reorganisation of work. In B. Burchell, D. Lapido, & F. Wilkinson (Eds.), *Job insecurity and work intensification* (pp. 39–60). London: Routledge.

Innocenti, L., Pilati, M., & Peluso, A. M. (2011). Trust as moderator in the relationship between HRM practices and employee attitudes. *Human Resource Management Journal, 21*(3), 303–317.

James, L. R., Demaree, R. G., & Wolf, G. (1993). An assessment of within-group interrater agreement. *Journal of Applied Psychology, 78,* 306–339.

Jiang, L., & Probst, T. M. (2015). Do your employees (collectively) trust you? The importance of trust climate beyond individual trust. *Scandinavian Journal of Management, 31*(4), 526–535.

Kahn-Freund, O. (1954). The legal framework. In A. Flanders & H. Clegg (Eds.), *The system of industrial relations in Great Britain* (pp. 42–127). Oxford: Blackwell.

Keim, A. C., Landis, R. S., Pierce, C. A., & Earnest, D. R. (2014). Why do employees worry about their jobs? A meta-analytic review of predictors of job insecurity. *Journal of Occupational Health Psychology, 19*(3), 269–290.

Klug, K. (2017). Young and at risk? Consequences of job insecurity for mental health and satisfaction among labor market entrants with different levels of education. *Economic and Industrial Democracy,* first published online. doi:10.1177/0143831X17731609

Kuenzi, M., & Schminke, M. (2009). Assembling fragments into a lens: A review, critique, and proposed research agenda for the organizational work climate literature. *Journal of Management, 35,* 634–717.

Lai, Y., Saridakis, G., Blackburn, R., & Johnstone, S. (2015). Are the HR responses of small firms different from large firms in times of recession? *Journal of Business Venturing, 31*(1), 113–131.

Lam, C. F., Liang, J., Ashford, S. J., & Lee, C. (2015). Job insecurity and organizational citizenship behavior: Exploring curvilinear and moderated relationships. *Journal of Applied Psychology, 100*(2), 499–510.

Langfred, C. W. (2004). Too much of a good thing? Negative effects of high trust and individual autonomy in self-managing teams. *Academy of Management Journal, 47*(3), 385–399.

Loi, R., Ngo, H. Y., Zhang, L. Q., & Lau, V. P. (2011). The interaction between leader- member exchange and perceived job security in predicting employee altruism and work performance. *Journal of Occupational and Organizational Psychology, 84,* 669–685.

Marchington, M., Wilkinson, A., Donnelly, R., & Kynighou, A. (2016). *Human resource management at work.* London: CIPD.

McEvily, B., Perrone, V., & Zaheer, A. (2003). Trust as an organizing principle. *Organization Science, 14* (1), 91–103.

Mishra, A. K., & Spreitzer, G. M. (1998). Explaining how survivors respond to downsizing: The roles of trust, empowerment, justice, and work redesign. *Academy of Management Review, 23*(3), 567–588.

Office for National Statistics (ONS). (2015). Employee contracts that do not guarantee a minimum number of hours – 2015 update, September, Retrieved from www.ons.org.uk

Peacock, L. (2013, February 20). One in seven workers made redundant since recession. *The Telegraph.* Retrieved from http://www.telegraph.co.uk/finance/jobs/9881215/One-in-seven-workers-made-redundant-since-recession.html

Public Sector Executive (PSE). (2016). Pay freeze and wage cap forcing public sector workers into debt, claim unions, 23.08.2016. Retrieved from http://www.publicsectorexecutive.com/News/pay-freeze-and-wage-cap-forcing-public-sector-workers-into-debt-claim-unions/148514

Pugh, S. D., Skarlicki, D. P., & Passell, B. S. (2003). After the fall: Layoff victims' trust and cynicism in re-employment. *Journal of Occupational Psychology, 76*(2), 2010–2212.

Rousseau, D. M., Sitkin, S. B., Burt, R. S., & Camerer, C. (1998). Not so different after all: A cross-discipline view of trust. *Academy of Management Review, 23*(3), 393–404.

Rubery, J. (2015). Change at work: Feminisation, flexibilisation, fragmentation and financialisation. *Employee Relations, 37*(6), 633–644.

Saridakis, G., Muñoz Torres, R., & Johnstone, S. (2013). Do human resource practices enhance organizational commitment in SMEs with low employee satisfaction? *British Journal of Management, 24* (3), 445–458.

Schilke, O., & Cook, K. S. (2013). A cross-level process theory of trust development in interorganizational relationships. *Strategic Organization, 11*(3), 281–303.

Schreurs, B., Guenter, H., van Emmerik, I. H., Notelaers, G., & Schumacher, D. (2015). Pay level satisfaction and employee outcomes: The moderating effect of autonomy and support climates. *The International Journal of Human Resource Management, 26*(12), 1523–1546.

Siebert, S., Martin, G., Bozic, B., & Docherty, I. (2015). Looking 'beyond the factory gates': Towards more pluralist and radical approaches to intraorganizational trust research. *Organization Studies, 36*(8), 1033–1062.

Snijders, T., & Bosker, R. (2012). Multilevel analysis. In *An introduction to basic and advanced multilevel modeling* (2nd ed.) (pp. 74–92). London: Sage Publications Inc.

Staufenbiel, T., & König, C. J. (2010). A model for the effects of job insecurity on performance, turnover intention, and absenteeism. *Journal of Occupational and Organizational Psychology, 83*(1), 101–117.

Sverke, M., Hellgren, J., & Näswall, K. (2002). No security: A meta-analysis and review of job insecurity and its consequences. *Journal of Occupational Health Psychology, 7*, 242–264.

Sverke, M., Hellgren, J., & Näswall, K. (2006). Job insecurity: A literature review. *Arbetslivsinstitutet.*

Timming, A. R. (2012). Tracing the effects of employee involvement and participation on trust in managers: An analysis of covariance structures. *International Journal of Human Resource Management, 23*(15), 3243–3257.

Tomer, J. F. (1987). *Organizational capital: The path to higher productivity and well- being.* New York: Praeger.

Truss, C., Mankin, D., & Kellinher, C. (2012). *Strategic human resource management.* Oxford: OUP.

Wang, W., & Heyes, J. (2017). Flexibility, flexicurity and labour productivity. *International Journal of Human Resource Management, 23*, 1–21.

Wang, W., & Seifert, R. (2017). Pay reductions and work attitudes: The moderating effect of employee involvement practices. *Employee Relations, 39*(7), 935–950.

Warr, P. (1990). The measurement of well-being and other aspects of mental health. *Journal of Occupational Psychology, 63*, 193–210.

Wedderburn (Lord). (1986). *The worker and the Law* (3rd ed.). Harmondsworth: Penguin.

Whitener, E. M. (2001). Do 'high commitment' human resource practices affect employee commitment? A cross-level analysis using hierarchical linear modelling. *Journal of Management, 27*, 515–535.

Wong, Y. T., Wong, C. S., Ngo, H. Y., & Lui, H. K. (2005). Different responses to job insecurity of Chinese workers in joint ventures and state-owned enterprises. *Human Relations, 58*, 1391–1418.

Wood, S., Van Veldhoven, M., Croon, M., & de Menezes, L. M. (2012). Enriched job design, high involvement management and organizational performance: The mediating roles of job satisfaction and well-being. *Human Relations, 65*(4), 419–445.

Workplace Employment Relations Study for 2011, Gov.UK. (2014). Retrieved from https://www.gov.uk/government/publications/the-2011-workplace-employment-relations-study-wers

Trust development across levels of analysis: An embedded-agency perspective

Fabrice Lumineau and Oliver Schilke

ABSTRACT

This article advances a cross-level model of trust development. Drawing upon an embedded-agency perspective from institutional theory, we combine a top-down with a bottom-up approach, reflecting the inherent duality of trust in organisational settings. Specifically, we elaborate a reciprocal process that illustrates how organisational structures influence individuals' trust and, at the same time, how individuals' trust manifests in organisational structures. We discuss the theoretical implications of our cross-level model for the trust literature and propose important avenues for future research.

Introduction

Over the last three decades, the scholarly literature has paid much attention to the question of trust development (Child & Möllering, 2003; Cook & Schilke, 2010; Williams, 2001). This body of work has focused, for instance, on how trust – defined as confident positive expectations regarding another's conduct (Lewicki, McAllister, & Bies, 1998) – develops among individuals (e.g. Lander & Kooning, 2013; Lewicki, Tomlinson, & Gillespie, 2006) or among organisations (e.g. Graebner, Lumineau, & Fudge Kamal, forthcoming; Malhotra & Lumineau, 2011; Zhang, Viswanathan, & Henke, 2011). However, trust has traditionally been analyzed at one single level of analysis at a time (Fulmer & Gelfand, 2012). As a result, much theorising on trust has been biased toward either overly individualist or overly structural accounts (Kroeger, 2012; Lewis & Weigert, 1985). The former type of account treats trust as a strictly individual phenomenon and often conceptualises interpersonal trust in a vacuum, thus stripping it from the broader social and organisational context in which it is embedded. Conversely, the latter suffers from a simplistic focus on the broader preconditions for trust and fails to shed light on individuals' agency and the mechanisms through which trust develops. Either focus is problematic when studying trust in organisational settings, because both types fail to reflect the fact that organisations are inherently multi-level entities.

In this article, we draw and expand upon recent research emphasising the important multi-level nature of trust (e.g. Currall & Inkpen, 2002; Fulmer & Gelfand, 2012; Gillespie & Dietz, 2009; Schilke & Cook, 2013) to analyze the reciprocal relationship between the individual and organisational levels in trust development. We first affirm the need for more multi-level trust research and introduce an embedded-agency perspective as a guiding framework for the analysis of cross-level trust development. Second, we advance a multi-level model of trust development. We start by analysing how organisational structures influence individuals' trust and then turn to an analysis of how individuals' trust can manifest in organisational structures. Finally, we discuss the theoretical implications of our multi-level model of trust development for the trust literature and propose important avenues for future research.

The need for more multi-level trust research

Despite the great volume of scholarly work on trust, only a relatively small substream of this research has been interested in the issue of trust across levels of analysis (see Fulmer & Gelfand, 2012 for a review). Most work has focused on trust either at the individual level (e.g. Robinson, 1996; Rotter, 1967) or at the organisational level (e.g. Doney & Cannon, 1997; Schilke & Cook, 2015). However, we still know relatively little about how trust develops *across* levels of analysis and how micro and macro features of trust are interrelated. The relative deficiency of theoretical developments specific to trust development across levels is problematic because 'findings at one level of analysis do not generalise neatly and exactly to other levels of analysis' (Klein & Kozlowski, 2000, p. 213). Trust scholars should therefore be particularly careful about a lurking cross-level fallacy (Rousseau, 1985; Rousseau & House, 1994) and clearly articulate how trust dynamics operate at and across distinct levels of analysis. They should pay attention to the possibility of using theories initially developed at the individual level at the organisational level, and vice versa (Dansereau & Yammarino, 2005) to determine whether isomorphism exists among trust constructs at different levels of analysis (Rousseau, 1985). For example, as suggested by macro scholars (Gulati & Nickerson, 2008; Zaheer & Harris, 2006), trust at the organisational level may be more than the simple sum of individuals' trust; as such, the analysis of trust at the organisational level should avoid unreflected anthropormorphizations of organisations. Moreover, failing to explicitly acknowledge that trust can exist at multiple levels precludes insight into relevant processes that span across levels.

In this article, we argue that trust is inherently a multi-level phenomenon and, thus, that our understanding of trust development should embrace the reciprocal relationships between micro and macro perspectives. We thus advance a multi-level model of trust development that combines bottom-up and top-down processes. This approach allows us to articulate how trust at lower ('micro') levels of analysis may be affected by higher ('macro') level entities and, vice versa, how trust at higher levels of analysis can emerge from lower level entities. As such, to understand trust development across levels more fully, it is important to account for its duality. In the following sections, we discuss the interactive influence between individual and organisational levels throughout the process of trust development, as summarised in Figure 1. We first introduce the notion of embedded agency as an organising principle for our trust development model before elaborating the reciprocal effects of trust at the individual and organisational levels.

Embedded agency

A framework explicitly addressing the bidirectional relations between individuals and organisations follows the embedded-agency approach (Barley & Tolbert, 1997;

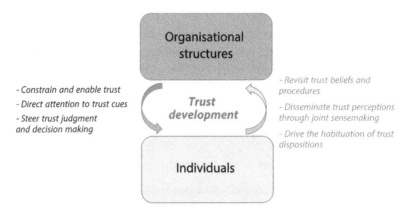

Figure 1. A multi-level model of trust development.

Seo 2002) that is at the heart of current inquiry in institutional theory (Garud, Hardy, & Maguire, 2007; Harmon, Haack, & Roulet, forthcoming). Traditionally, institutional theorists one-sidedly focused on how broader institutions constrain lower-level action, but more recently they have come to agree that both institutional structure and individual agency matter and are in a reciprocal relationship (Cardinale, 2018). Applying an organisations-as-institutions perspective (Tolbert, 1988; Zucker, 1983) and zooming in on the organisational and individual levels, the idea of embedded agency implies the existence of two types of concurrent cross-level effects: top-down (i.e. organisation→individuals) and bottom-up (individuals→organisation).

Top-down

Organisational structures that are taken for granted and describe reality for the organisation specify and justify its members' cognition and behaviours (Garud et al., 2007). Organisational rules, norms, and beliefs function as performance scripts that offer guideposts on how to think and behave when acting within the limits or on behalf of the organisation. Conformity with organisational structures provides actors legitimacy, whereas deviations from these prescriptions are thought to be counteracted by sanctions or are costly in some other manner (Jepperson, 1991). Moreover, shared cognitive frames at the organisational level provide a common understanding of situations and give joint meaning to ambiguous situations, such that the perception of these situations tends to converge among organisational members (Weick, 1979). Consequently, organisational structures may both constrain (make impossible) and enable (make possible) some actions and, over time, may even imprint certain dispositions that orient action (Cardinale, 2018; DiMaggio, 1988). As a result, individual behaviour and perception can be understood as being shaped by organisational structures.

Bottom-up

On the other hand, organisational structures are not fixed but are created and can be disrupted by the individuals enacting them (DiMaggio, 1988; Emirbayer & Mische, 1998; Holm, 1995). It is particularly when individual actors are temporally confronted with different structural environments or when the current structure proves highly ineffective that they may come to contest the status quo (Emirbayer & Mische, 1998). Moreover, new-comers who have not yet been fully socialised into the organisation may also be prone to questioning current organisational structures (Tolbert, 1988). In all these situations, indi-viduals may come to break with existing organisational structures and start to institutio-nalise new rules and behaviours. It is through individuals' interactions and shared sense making that new organisational structures may come into being (Cornelissen, Durand, Fiss, Lammers, & Vaara, 2015), in turn affecting organisational members' future cognition and behaviour.

In summary, the notion of embedded agency stresses how macro-level meanings, such as organisational structures, can make their way into micro-level cognition and behaviour, as well as how, vice versa, micro-level phenomena can build up to either further maintain or change macro-level structures. We apply this general idea to the specific realm of trust and develop the position that trust at the organisational level and trust at the individual level are mutually embedded.

How organisational structures influence individuals' trust

Here, we adopt a broad understanding of organisational structures to encompass both formal organisational design and informal organisational norms and procedures (Cao & Lumineau, 2015). Most generally, the design of an organisation's structure refers to 'the pattern of communications and relations among a group of human beings, including the processes for making and implementing decisions' (Simon, 1947, pp. 18–19). Within an organisation, such structures manifest, for instance, through the ways responsibilities are separated, division of labour is supported, tasks are designed, power is distributed, or incentives are organised. In inter-organisational relationships, for example, organis-ational design operates most notably through contracts and administrative controls (Gulati, Puranam, & Tushman, 2012; Schilke & Lumineau, 2018).

In addition to a formal governance system of polices and plans, organisational structure also manifests through informal channels. Informal structures affect trusting and trust-worthiness behaviour not only directly, by delineating appropriate behaviours, but also indirectly, by shaping beliefs and expectations (Denison, 1996; Lumineau & Malhotra, 2011; Schilke & Cook, 2015). These structures create norms, which guide actors' behaviour and specify permissible limits (Ouchi, 1979). In addition, informal structures support a logic of action, or interaction pattern, through which individuals evaluate each other's behav-iour and the appropriateness of their own response (Schilke, 2018). They represent a col-lectively shared way of making sense of social cues (Fainshmidt & Frazier, 2017).

This set of both formal and informal organisational design aspects influences how boundedly rational individuals focus their scarce attention and interpret informational cues (Schilke, 2018). Consistent with the information-processing view (Galbraith, 1974; Schilke & Lumineau, 2018; Thompson, 1967; Tushman & Nadler, 1978), we propose that judgments and decision making underlying trust development are influenced by organis-ational structures that guide selective attention to organisational issues. Organisational structures shape the nature of the actions taken by individuals to gather information when making decisions about trust. That is, they orient how managers and employees within an organisation gather cues and draw inferences about trustworthiness.

Organisational structures also influence the way information is interpreted and how individuals make sense of its importance (Cyert & March, 1963).

Lumineau (2017) applies this logic specifically to the influence of contracts – as an important type of formal organisational structure – on individuals' trust formation processes. He argues that the type of contract design – through its respective focus on controlling and coordinating aspects – induces specific calculative and noncalculative mechanisms behind the development of trust. For instance, Lumineau (2017, p. 1560) suggests that:

> Contractual control, through its focus on the definition on the acceptable behaviors in the relationship and the penalties in case of violation of these rules, enables partners to make a more accurate assessment of the risks and the payoffs. It helps parties to assess the risks with the potential gain for the trustor and the trustor's potential loss if the trustee does not fulfill its expectations (Coleman, 1990). As such, contractual control increases the type of information necessary to make a deliberative cost-benefit analysis, which is the basic mechanism behind calculative decision making. [...] By reinforcing the probabilistic side of decision making and the informational requirements to deal with risk, contractual control supports trust involving calculative judgments.

Similarly, *informal* organisational structures can play a significant role in individuals' trust formation processes. As individuals in organisations come together to determine the trustworthiness of a target (e.g. of a particular prominent person, the organisation itself, or another organisation), they engage in joint sense making efforts that, over time, become habitualized and taken for granted. In this way, not only the procedures that go into trustworthiness assessments, but also certain trust judgments themselves, diffuse and converge across individuals (Barley & Tolbert, 1997). For example, individual organisational members may come to learn that, we – as an organisation – are generally suspicious of outsiders, tend not to share privileged information with other organisations, and ultimately prefer not to trust third parties when we can avoid it. Organisational trust can thus become highly institutionalised. To a certain degree, it can even become independent of the individuals involved and thus remain stable even though individuals may change (Kroeger, 2012; Schilke & Cook, 2013). In this view, organisational trust can become an intersubjective phenomenon that is reflected in a collective orientation (Ferrin, Bligh, & Kohles, 2007; Zaheer, McEvily, & Perrone, 1998) – an informal organisational structure that can substantially affect the trust formation of organisational members and that can last over relatively long periods of time (Janowicz-Panjaitan & Noorderhaven, 2009).

We thus suggest that by inducing specific information-processing and decision-making mechanisms, organisational structures substantially influence (i.e. either constrain or enable) trust development at the individual level of the organisational member. Both formal and informal structures work as perceptual filters that direct employee attention to relevant trust cues. They influence how individual actors collect, process, and distribute information. Specifically, organisational structures guide individuals at different stages during the formation of their expectations. First, structures shape the motivation to share information (i.e. motivational mechanisms). Second, structures shape what information is attended to and how attention to problems and alternatives is sustained (i.e. attentional mechanisms). Third, structures shape the interpretation of information (i.e. interpretive mechanisms), steering trust judgment and decision making. Organisational structures are therefore critical factors guiding how individuals recognise and notice potential issues (i.e. focus of attention), diagnose situations (i.e. problem representation and formulation), search for solutions (i.e. deliberation and reflection), and screen different alternatives regarding trust.

How individuals' trust manifests in organisational structures

In addition to the top-down effect, we also consider how individuals' trust perceptions can 'spiral up' and diffuse from the individual to the organisational level. While organisational members' trust deliberations may of course be informed by relevant organisational structures (as discussed above), we can envision several scenarios in which these structures have only limited effects. For instance, newcomers to an organisation or individuals low in organisational identification may be ignorant of, or deliberately resist, organisational norms for trust formation. Moreover, when it comes to evaluating a novel trust target for which no pre-existing organisational-level trust judgment is readily available or a target that calls for a significant recalibration of trust (e.g. due to a blatant breach of trust), the novelty of the situation may require stepping outside established organisational templates, thus opening up the potential for individual-level dispositions and preferences to play an important role in the trust assessment process. To the extent that these individual dispositions and preferences are distinct from those of the broader organisation, the focal individual may use trust formation heuristics that differ from those commonly employed by the organisation and/or may ultimately come to divergent trust assessments. With existing organisational structures no longer fully determining the trust formation process, the individual may thus begin to break with existing organisational procedures and – perhaps unknowingly – start to develop a new pattern of trust formation routines.

Having formed her own trust beliefs, the individual will start to engage in workplace interactions and begin to disseminate these beliefs to other organisational members. At this stage, the individual's deviating trust beliefs may collide with established organisational norms held by these other organisational members. The outcome of the tension between individual- and organisational-level dispositions will depend, among other things, on the focal individual's social influence in the organisation. Specifically, in order for divergent trust beliefs to make it from the individual to the organisational level, the opinions of the individual must be visible to the broader organisation, and the organisation must value those opinions (Friedkin, 1993). For example, the focal individual's confidence in her trust judgment, her personal skills in pitching her trust beliefs to coworkers, the strength of her connections to important other members in the organisation, and more broadly her power, charisma, and status will affect whether or not her trust belief will be able to diffuse to the organisational level.

To the extent that the new trust belief successfully spreads within the organisation, it may over time come to be seen as an objective truth, and new behavioural routines consistent with this truth will emerge. In other words, trust habituates and becomes ingrained in revised patterns of behaviour in the organisation. At this point, the revised trust belief has obtained a certain firmness and can no longer be readily changed by any single individual, which is why we may speak of organisational-level trust at this point (Schilke & Cook, 2013).

There is also evidence that, beyond their effect on the emergence of informal trust structures at the organisational level, individuals play a significant role in shaping formal organisational structures related to trust. In particular, Vlaar, Van den Bosch, and Volberda (2007) convincingly argue that individuals' experiences, especially at the beginning of a relationship with a new trust target, can have long-lasting imprints on the organisational structures put in place to govern that relationship. Especially when individuals come to experience a target as distrustful, they will advocate for formal control mechanisms to be put in place, while initially experienced trust reduces the perceived need for such mechanisms. Strong formalisation and control, once put into place, may obviate the need for further trust development in subsequent relationship stages and may even act as a signal to other organisational members that the target should not be trusted (Lumineau, 2017; Malhotra & Lumineau, 2011; Poppo & Zenger, 2002). As such, individuals' initial trust perceptions may translate to the organisational level through formal structures, such as formalisation and control.

Overall, we thus suggest that individual organisational members can shape trust at the organisational level. Individuals may, under certain circumstances, come to revisit existing organisational trust beliefs and procedures. Subsequently, new trust perceptions may diffuse from these individuals to the broader organisation through joint sensemaking mechanisms. Ultimately, this bottom-up process may result in the habituation of revised trust dispositions.

Discussion and future research

Drawing on an embedded agency perspective, we advocate a cross-level analysis of trust development that links the individual and organisational levels within the same conceptual framework to show how and why micro and macro factors do not work in isolation but are fundamentally intertwined. For analytical purposes, we organised our argumentation around a distinction between top-down and bottom-up processes, although we acknowledge that these two types of processes may occur simultaneously. It is clear that we are only at an early stage of studying trust across levels of analyses, and we encourage future research of both empirical and conceptual nature to test and expand our framework.

In addition to issues of concomitance, one problem that empirical investigation of our model may face is the issue of causality between individual and organisational factors. We suspect that scholars willing to disentangle which of these sets of factors come first may face many operational challenges. In this respect, we believe that an experimental approach will be particularly promising to help trust scholars establish causality by eliminating extraneous factors and endogeneity issues (Bitektine, Lucas, & Schilke, 2018). Experimental methods can also be particularly useful for separating reciprocal effects, as the recent study by Døjbak Håkonsson et al. (2016) nicely exemplifies.

Another line of inquiry to extend our multi-level model is to pay greater attention to the dynamic aspects of trust development as it unfolds over time. It would be especially interesting to investigate the risk of vicious cycles, where a minor reduction of trust at one level translates into a heightened change at another level, which in turn leads to progressively greater reductions in trust. For example, negative expectations may lead individuals to develop rigid and prevention-focused structures, which can foster self-fulfilling prophecies (Ghoshal & Moran, 1996). Clearly, we need to better understand how to prevent the development of such vicious cycles of progressive trust destruction. Research into trust cycles may raise interesting questions regarding the possibility to 'reboot' a relationship to either stop a spiral of trust reduction – through, for instance, a change of boundary spanners or the renegotiation of formal agreement (Brattström, Faems, & Mahring, 2018) – or to restart trust building by overcoming existing inertia at the individual and/or organisational level.

For the sake of parsimony, our multi-level model focuses on the development of trust. However, in line with research distinguishing trust and distrust as two distinct constructs (Guo, Lumineau, & Lewicki, 2017; Lewicki et al., 1998; Luhmann, 1979), we see many opportunities to extend our analysis to integrate the development of distrust across levels of analysis. Indeed, as suggested by recent research (Bijlsma-Frankema, Sitkin, & Weibel, 2015; Dimoka, 2010; Lumineau, 2017; Reimann, Schilke, & Cook, 2017), it is likely that the mechanisms underlying the dynamics of trust and distrust development differ fundamentally.

Another promising way to expand our model, with its focus on the individual and organisational levels, is for future research to introduce additional levels of analysis, such as the team or the country level. Such an approach, we believe, would fruitfully extend and enrich the logic deployed in this article.

Finally, we encourage future research to analyze the contextual factors that might strengthen or weaken the mechanisms suggested in our multi-level model of trust development. For instance, we call for research on how the mechanisms described in our model may operate across different types of individuals and different types of organisations. Individuals' training, psychological traits, demographic background, education, or (official and unofficial) status within the organisation are likely to influence the nature of the processes underlying trust development. Moreover, certain types of organisations may be more open to change in their trust dispositions and routines through individuals, whereas such disruptions will be harder to achieve in other organisations.

We believe the time is ripe for trust scholarship to advance our multi-level understanding of trust. Such inquiries would particularly benefit from more collaboration among micro and macro trust scholars (Polzer, Gulati, Khurana, & Tushman, 2009). As we demonstrated here, trust is a complex construct that cannot be reduced to individual behaviours, nor can it be fully explained through organisational structures. We hope our cross-level model of trust development provides an impetus for further exploration of the processes, interactions, and dynamics enacted by organisational actors and contexts across multiple levels.

Disclosure statement

No potential conflict of interest was reported by the authors.

References

Barley, S. R., & Tolbert, P. S. (1997). Institutionalization and structuration: Studying the links between action and institution. *Organization Studies, 18*(1), 93–117.

Bijlsma-Frankema, K., Sitkin, S. B., & Weibel, A. (2015). Distrust in the balance: The emergence and development of intergroup distrust in a court of law. *Organization Science, 26*(4), 1018–1039.

Bitektine, A., Lucas, J. W., & Schilke, O. (2018). Institutions under a microscope: Experimental methods in institutional theory. In A. Bryman & D. A. Buchanan (Eds.), *Unconventional methodology in organization and management research* (pp. 147–167). Oxford: Oxford University Press.

Brattström, A., Faems, D., & Mahring, M. (2018). From trust convergence to trust divergence: Trust development in conflictual interorganizational relationships. *Organization Studies*, forthcoming.

Cao, Z., & Lumineau, F. (2015). Revisiting the interplay between contractual and relational governance: A qualitative and meta-analytic investigation. *Journal of Operations Management, 33-34*, 15–42.

Cardinale, I. (2018). Beyond constraining and enabling: Toward new microfoundations for institutional theory. *Academy of Management Review, 43*(1), 132–155.

Child, J., & Möllering, G. (2003). Contextual confidence and active trust development in the Chinese business environment. *Organization Science, 14*, 69–80.

Cook, K. S., & Schilke, O. (2010). The role of public, relational and organizational trust in economic affairs. *Corporate Reputation Review, 13*(2), 98–109.

Cornelissen, J. P., Durand, R., Fiss, P. C., Lammers, J. C., & Vaara, E. (2015). Putting communication front and center in institutional theory and analysis. *Academy of Management Review, 40*(1), 10–27.

Coleman, J. S. (1990). *Foundations of social theory*. Cambridge, MA: Harvard University Press.

Currall, S. C., & Inkpen, A. C. (2002). A multilevel approach to trust in joint ventures. *Journal of International Business Studies, 33*(3), 479–495.

Cyert, R. M., & March, J. G. (1963). *A behavioral theory of the firm*. Englewood Cliffs, NJ: Prentice-Hall.

Dansereau, F., & Yammarino, F. J. (2005). *Multi-level issues in strategy and methods*. Amsterdam: Emerald.

Denison, D. R. (1996). What is the difference between organizational culture and organizational climate? A native's point of view on a decade of paradigm wars. *Academy of Management Review, 21*(3), 619–654.

DiMaggio, P. (1988). Interest and agency in institutional theory. In L. G. Zucker (Ed.), *Institutional patterns and organizations: Culture and environment* (pp. 3–21). Cambridge, MA: Ballinger.

Dimoka, A. (2010). What does the brain tell us about trust and distrust? Evidence from a functional neuroimaging study. *MIS Quarterly, 34*, 373–396.

Døjbak Håkonsson, D., Eskildsen, J. K., Argote, L., Mønster, D., Burton, R. M., & Obel, B. (2016). Exploration versus exploitation: Emotions and performance as antecedents and consequences of team decisions. *Strategic Management Journal, 37*(6), 985–1001.

Doney, P. M., & Cannon, J. P. (1997). An examination of the nature of trust in buyer-seller relationships. *Journal of Marketing, 61*(2), 35–51.

Emirbayer, M., & Mische, A. (1998). What is agency? *American Journal of Sociology, 103*(4), 962–1023.

Fainshmidt, S., & Frazier, M. L. (2017). What facilitates dynamic capabilities? The role of organizational climate for trust. *Long Range Planning, 50*(5), 550–566.

Ferrin, D. L., Bligh, M. C., & Kohles, J. C. (2007). Can I trust you to trust me? A theory of trust, monitoring, and cooperation in interpersonal and intergroup relationships. *Group & Organization Management, 32*(4), 465–499.

Friedkin, N. E. (1993). Structural bases of interpersonal influence in groups: A longitudinal case study. *American Sociological Review, 58*(6), 861–872.

Fulmer, C. A., & Gelfand, M. J. (2012). At what level (and in whom) we trust: Trust across multiple organizational levels. *Journal of Management, 38*(4), 1167–1230.

Galbraith, J. R. (1974). Organization design: An information processing view. *Interfaces, 4*(3), 28–36.

Garud, R., Hardy, C., & Maguire, S. (2007). Institutional entrepreneurship as embedded agency: An introduction to the special issue. *Organization Studies, 28*(7), 957–969.

Ghoshal, S., & Moran, P. (1996). Bad for practice: A critique of the transaction cost theory. *Academy of Management Review, 21*, 13–47.

Gillespie, N., & Dietz, G. (2009). Trust repair after an organization-level failure. *Academy of Management Review, 34*(1), 127–145.

Graebner, M., Lumineau, F., & Fudge Kamal, D. (forthcoming). Unrequited: Asymmetry in interorganizational trust. *Strategic Organization.*

Gulati, R., & Nickerson, J. (2008). Interorganizational trust, governance choice, and exchange performance. *Organization Science, 19*, 688–708.

Gulati, R., Puranam, P., & Tushman, M. (2012). Meta-organization design: Rethinking design in inter-organizational and community contexts. *Strategic Management Journal, 33*(6), 571–586.

Guo, S. L., Lumineau, F., & Lewicki, R. (2017). Revisiting the foundations of organizational distrust. *Foundations and Trends® in Management, 1*(1), 1–88.

Harmon, D. J., Haack, P., & Roulet, T. J. (forthcoming). Microfoundations of institutions: A matter of structure vs. agency or level of analysis? *Academy of Management Review.*

Holm, P. (1995). The dynamics of institutionalization: Transformation processes in Norwegian fisheries. *Administrative Science Quarterly, 40*(3), 398–422.

Janowicz-Panjaitan, M., & Noorderhaven, N. G. (2009). Trust, calculation, and interorganizational learning of tacit knowledge: An organizational roles perspective. *Organization Studies, 30*(10), 1021–1044.

Jepperson, R. L. (1991). Institutions, institutional effects, and institutionalization. In W. W. Powell & P. J. DiMaggio (Eds.), *The new institutionalism in organizational analysis* (pp. 143–163). Chicago, IL: University of Chicago Press.

Klein, K. J., & Kozlowski, S. W. J. (2000). From micro to meso: Critical steps in conceptualizing and conducting multilevel research. *Organizational Research Methods, 3*(4), 211–236.

Kroeger, F. (2012). Trusting organizations: The institutionalization of trust in interorganizational relationships. *Organization, 19*(6), 743–763.

Lander, M. W., & Kooning, L. (2013). Boarding the aircraft: Trust development amongst negotiators of a complex merger. *Journal of Management Studies, 50*(1), 1–30.

Lewicki, R. J., McAllister, D. J., & Bies, R. J. (1998). Trust and distrust: New relationships and realities. *Academy of Management Review, 23*, 438–458.

Lewicki, R. J., Tomlinson, E., & Gillespie, N. (2006). Models of interpersonal trust development: Theoretical approaches, empirical evidence, and future directions. *Journal of Management, 32*, 991–1022.

Lewis, J. D., & Weigert, A. (1985). Trust as a social reality. *Social Forces, 63*(4), 967–985.

Luhmann, N. (1979). *Trust and power.* New York: Wiley.

Lumineau, F. (2017). How contracts influence trust and distrust. *Journal of Management, 43*(5), 1553–1577.

Lumineau, F., & Malhotra, D. (2011). Shadow of the contract: How contract structure shapes interfirm dispute resolution. *Strategic Management Journal, 32*(5), 532–555.

Malhotra, D., & Lumineau, F. (2011). Trust and collaboration in the aftermath of conflict: The effects of contract structure. *Academy of Management Journal, 54*(5), 981–998.

Ouchi, W. G. (1979). A conceptual framework for the design of organizational control mechanisms. *Management Science, 25*(9), 833–848.

Polzer, J. T., Gulati, R., Khurana, R., & Tushman, M. L. (2009). Crossing boundaries to increase relevance in organizational research. *Journal of Management Inquiry, 18*(4), 280–286.

Poppo, L., & Zenger, T. (2002). Do formal contracts and relational governance function as substitutes or complements? *Strategic Management Journal, 23*(8), 707–725.

Reimann, M., Schilke, S., & Cook, K. S. (2017). Trust is heritable, whereas distrust is not. *Proceedings of the National Academy of Sciences, 114*(27), 7007–7012.

Robinson, S. L. (1996). Trust and breach of the psychological contract. *Administrative Science Quarterly, 41*(4), 574–599.

Rotter, J. B. (1967). A new scale for the measurement of interpersonal trust. *Journal of Personality, 35* (4), 651–665.

Rousseau, D. M. (1985). Issues of level in organizational research: Multi-level and cross-level perspectives. *Research in Organizational Behavior, 7*(1), 1–37.

Rousseau, D. M., & House, R. J. (1994). Meso organizational behavior: Avoiding three fundamental biases. *Journal of Organizational Behavior, 1*(1), 13–30.

Schilke, O. (2018). A micro-institutional inquiry into resistance to environmental pressures. *Academy of Management Journal, 61*(4), 1431–1466.

Schilke, O., & Cook, K. S. (2013). A cross-level process theory of trust development in interorganizational relationships. *Strategic Organization, 11*, 281–303.

Schilke, O., & Cook, K. S. (2015). Sources of alliance partner trustworthiness: Integrating calculative and relational perspectives. *Strategic Management Journal, 36*(2), 276–297.

Schilke, O., & Lumineau, F. (2018). The double-edged effect of contracts on alliance performance. *Journal of Management, 44*(7), 2827–2858.

Seo, M.-G., & Creed, W. E. (2002). Institutional contradictions, praxis, and institutional change: A dialectical perspective. *Academy of Management Review, 27*(2), 222–247.

Simon, H. A. (1947). *Administrative behavior: A study of decision-making processes in administrative organization*. New York, NY: Macmillan.

Thompson, J. D. (1967). *Organizations in action: Social science bases of administrative theory*. New York, NY: McGraw-Hill.

Tolbert, P. S. (1988). Institutional sources of organizational culture in major law firms. In L. G. Zucker (Ed.), *Institutional patterns and organizations: Culture and environment* (pp. 101–113). Cambridge, MA: Ballinger.

Tushman, M. L., & Nadler, D. A. (1978). Information processing as an integrating concept in organizational design. *Academy of Management Review, 3*(3), 613–624.

Vlaar, P. W. L., Van den Bosch, F. A. J., & Volberda, H. W. (2007). On the evolution of trust, distrust, and formal coordination and control in interorganizational relationships: Toward an integrative framework. *Group & Organization Management, 32*(4), 407–428.

Weick, K. (1979). *The social psychology of organizing*. New York, NY: Random House.

Williams, M. (2001). In whom we trust: Group membership as an affective context for trust development. *Academy of Management Review, 26*(3), 377–396.

Zaheer, A., & Harris, J. (2006). Interorganizational trust. In O. Shenkar & J. J. Reuer (Eds.), *Handbook of strategic alliances* (pp. 169–197). Thousand Oaks, CA: Sage.

Zaheer, A., McEvily, B., & Perrone, V. (1998). Does trust matter? Exploring the effects of interorganizational and interpersonal trust on performance. *Organization Science, 9*(2), 141–159.

Zhang, C., Viswanathan, S., & Henke, J. W. (2011). The boundary spanning capabilities of purchasing agents in buyer-supplier trust development. *Journal of Operations Management, 29*(4), 318–328.

Zucker, L. G. (1983). Organizations as institutions. *Research in the Sociology of Organizations, 2*, 1–47.

Index